Optimizing Windows® 7

Pocket Consultant

William R. Stanek
Author and Series Editor

PUBLISHED BY
Microsoft Press
A Division of Microsoft Corporation
One Microsoft Way
Redmond, Washington 98052-6399

Library of Congress Control Number: 2011934421
ISBN: 978-0-7356-6165-3

Printed and bound in the United States of America.

First Printing

Microsoft Press books are available through booksellers and distributors worldwide. If
you need support related to this book, email Microsoft Press Book Support at mspinput@
microsoft.com. Please tell us what you think of this book at http://www.microsoft.com/
learning/booksurvey.

Microsoft and the trademarks listed at http://www.microsoft.com/about/legal/en/us/
IntellectualProperty/Trademarks/EN-US.aspx are trademarks of the Microsoft group of
companies. All other marks are property of their respective owners.

The example companies, organizations, products, domain names, email addresses, logos,
people, places, and events depicted herein are fictitious. No association with any real
company, organization, product, domain name, email address, logo, person, place, or event
is intended or should be inferred.

This book expresses the author's views and opinions. The information contained in this
book is provided without any express, statutory, or implied warranties. Neither the authors,
Microsoft Corporation, nor its resellers, or distributors will be held liable for any damages
caused or alleged to be caused either directly or indirectly by this book.

Acquisitions Editor: Jeff Koch
Developmental Editor: Karen Szall
Project Editor: Rosemary Caperton
Editorial Production: Christian Holdener, S4Carlisle Publishing Services
Technical Reviewer: Bob Hogan; Technical Review services provided by Content Master,
a member of CM Group, Ltd.
Copyeditor: Crystal Thomas
Indexer: Jean Skipp
Cover: Twist Creative · Seattle

Contents

What do you think of this book? We want to hear from you!

Microsoft is interested in hearing your feedback so we can continually improve our
books and learning resources for you. To participate in a brief online survey, please visit:

microsoft.com/learning/booksurvey

Chapter 3   Customizing Boot, Startup, and Power Options   45

Chapter 4   Organizing, Searching, and Indexing   67

What do you think of this book? We want to hear from you!

Microsoft is interested in hearing your feedback so we can continually improve our books and learning resources for you. To participate in a brief online survey, please visit:

microsoft.com/learning/booksurvey

Introduction

Welcome to *Optimizing Windows 7 Pocket Consultant*. Over the years, I've written about many different Windows technologies and products, but one of the products I like writing about most is Windows itself. When you start working with Windows 7, you'll see at once that this operating system is visually different from earlier releases of Windows. What won't be readily apparent, however, is just how different—and that's because many of the most significant changes to the operating system are under the surface. These changes affect the underlying architecture, not just the interfaces—and they were some of the hardest for me to research and write about.

In this book, I teach you how features work, why they work the way they do, and how to customize them to meet your needs. I also offer specific examples of how certain features can meet your needs and how you can use other features to troubleshoot and resolve issues you might have. In addition, this book provides tips, best practices, and examples of how to fine-tune all major aspects of Windows 7. This book won't just teach you how to configure Windows 7; it will teach you how to squeeze every last bit of power out of it and make the most of the features and options it includes.

Who Is This Book For?

Optimizing Windows 7 Pocket Consultant covers all editions of Windows 7. The book is designed for the following readers:

- Accomplished users and information managers who want to know more about the operating system
- Administrators, help desk staff, and others who support the operating system
- Developers who develop applications for the operating system and want to know how to optimize core components

To pack in as much information as possible, I had to assume that you have basic networking skills and a basic understanding of Windows 7. I also assume that you are fairly familiar with Windows commands and procedures as well as the Windows user interface.

How Is This Book Organized?

Speed and ease of reference are essential parts of this hands-on guide. This book has an expanded table of contents and an extensive index for finding answers to problems quickly. Many other quick-reference features are included as well, including quick step-by-step procedures, lists, tables, and extensive cross-references.

Part I, "Optimization Essentials," focuses on fine-tuning the operating system's appearance and performance. No "Hello" and "Welcome" stuff here. You'll roll up your sleeves and dive right in to the good stuff while also learning how to personalize the operating system.

After you have customized the interface and appearance, *Optimizing Windows 7 Pocket Consultant* takes you through the process of optimizing core components. In Chapter 3, "Customizing Boot, Startup, and Power Options," you'll learn how to fine-tune boot, startup, power on, and resume. In Chapter 4, "Organizing, Searching, and Indexing," you'll learn how to optimally organize the documents, pictures, music, and other files on your computer so that you can not only get to them quickly but also view and work with them quickly. In Chapter 5, "Optimizing Your Computer's Software," you'll learn about managing and maintaining your computer's software with an emphasis on performance and problem resolution.

After you've fine-tuned the interface, appearance, and core components, you'll want to track system health and performance to ensure that your computer runs optimally—that's exactly what Part III, "Fine-Tuning Performance," covers. Here, you'll dig in and dive as deep as you want to into tracking, analyzing, and issue resolution.

Conventions Used In This Book

This book uses visual cues to help keep the text clear and easy to follow. You'll find code listings in monospace type, and text that you must type when performing a task appears in **boldface** type. New technical terms appear in *italics* and are followed by a definition.

Other Resources

Although some books are offered as all-in-one guides, there's simply no way one book can do it all. This book is intended to be used as a concise and easy-to-use resource. It covers everything you need to perform core optimization tasks for Windows 7, but it is by no means exhaustive.

As you encounter new topics, take the time to practice what you've learned and read about. Seek additional information as necessary to get the practical experience and knowledge that you need.

I recommend that you regularly visit the Microsoft website for Windows 7 (*http://www.microsoft.com/windows/*) and *http://support.microsoft.com* to stay current with the latest changes. You may also want to refer to *Windows 7 Administrator's Pocket Consultant* for more detailed information on management, maintenance, and problem resolution.

Support & Feedback

This section provides useful information about accessing any errata for this title, reporting errors and finding support, and providing feedback and contacting Microsoft Press.

Microsoft Press Errata and Support

We have made every effort to ensure the accuracy of this book and its companion content. Any errors that have been reported since this book was published are listed on our Microsoft Press site at oreilly.com:

> http://go.microsoft.com/FWLink/?Linkid=224294

If you find an error that is not already listed, you can report it to us through the same page.

If you need additional support, please email Microsoft Press Book Support at mspinput@microsoft.com.

Please note that product support for Microsoft software is not offered through the addresses above.

We Want to Hear from You

At Microsoft Press, your satisfaction is our top priority, and your feedback is our most valuable asset. Please tell us what you think of this book at:

> http://www.microsoft.com/learning/booksurvey

The survey is short, and we read *every one* of your comments and ideas. Thanks in advance for your input!

Stay in Touch

Let us keep the conversation going! We are on Twitter: *http://twitter.com/MicrosoftPress.*

William is on Twitter at *http://twitter.com/WilliamStanek* and on Facebook at *http://www.facebook.com/wstanek.*

CHAPTER 1

Customizing the Windows 7 Interface

Windows 7 is more customizable than any earlier release of the Windows operating system. Powerful new features and options combined with old favorites allow you to work in new ways. You can perform tasks more efficiently, and you can optimize and customize the operating system in many new and exciting ways.

Teaching you how to optimize Windows 7 and make it work the way you want it to is what this book is all about. If you were moving into a house, apartment, or dorm room, you would want to make the space your own. We do the same with just about everything in our lives, yet surprisingly few people take the time to make their virtual space their own, which can make using a computer a frustrating experience.

One of the ways to make Windows 7 your own is to customize the interface. In any operating system, the interface is everything that connects you to your computer and its basic elements, including the desktop, the menu system, and the taskbar. The way these basic elements look depends on appearance settings. The way they behave depends on customization settings saved in the user profile associated with a particular user account. Because your user account and its associated profile are separate from the profiles associated with other user accounts on a computer, you can customize the interface without affecting other users, and your preferred settings will be remembered and restored each time you log on.

Boosting Your Desktop IQ

The desktop is what you see after you start your computer and log on. It's your virtual workspace, and you must master it to begin using your computer faster and smarter.

Optimizing Interface Performance

Windows 7 (with the exception of Starter and Home Basic editions) supports Aero Glass features that provide desktop special effects such as blending and transparency. The Windows 7 desktop with Aero Glass enabled is pretty, but like any cosmetic, its value depends on many factors. The same can be said for the inessential animations and display effects that are enabled by default on most computers running Windows Home Premium or higher.

On older, less powerful computers, you will want to use less of the pretty stuff; using fewer system resources makes Windows more responsive. The same is likely to be true for that new netbook or tablet PC you just bought.

You can optimize the desktop for the way you want to work by following these steps:

1. Click Start, type **SystemPropertiesAdvanced** in the Search box, and then press Enter to open the System Properties dialog box with the Advanced tab selected.

    TIP Although there are many shortcuts you can use to access the various tabs and options of the System Properties dialog box, you need not know or remember them all. Instead, pick one technique you like, put it to memory, and use it. The technique I like most is the one mentioned in this step. If the Advanced tab isn't the one I want to work with after I've opened the dialog box, I simply click the tab I want to use, rather than trying to remember that SystemPropertiesComputerName opens the Computer Name tab, SystemPropertiesHardware opens the Hardware tab, SystemPropertiesProtection opens the System Protection tab, and SystemPropertiesRemote opens the Remote tab.

    REAL WORLD If command memorization isn't your thing but you'd still like a quick and easy way to access System Properties, try this: Click Start, and type SystemPropertiesAdvanced in the Search box on the Start menu. Right-click SystemPropertiesAdvanced in the results, and then click Pin To Taskbar. Now the System Properties | Advanced Tab shortcut is available on the taskbar. Whenever you want to access it, simply click the related icon on the taskbar.

2. In the Performance section, click Settings to open the Performance Options dialog box, shown in Figure 1-1. You can now:

    -   Select Adjust For Best Performance to get rid of all the pretty stuff, or select Adjust For Best Appearance to enable all the pretty stuff.
    -   Select or clear individual visual effects.

3. Save your changes by clicking OK twice to close both dialog boxes.

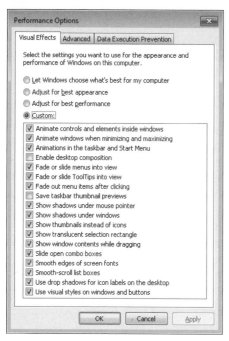

FIGURE 1-1 Configuring visual effects to optimize the desktop for the way you want to use it

The visual effects options that have the biggest effect on performance, in approximate order of impact, include:

- **Enable Transparent Glass** Controls Window transparency. This might be "flashy," but it is also resource intensive. When off, Windows and dialog box frames are solid.

- **Animate Windows When Minimizing And Maximizing** Determines whether squeezing or stretching animation is used when minimizing or maximizing windows. When off, Windows pop into position.

- **Fade Or Slide Menus Into View** Controls whether menus fade or slide into view. When off, menus snap open without delay.

- **Fade Or Slide ToolTips Into View** Controls whether tooltips fade or slide into view. When off, tooltips snap open without delay.

- **Animate Controls And Elements Inside Windows** Controls the slow-fade effect on buttons and tabs in dialog boxes. When off, buttons glow and tabs open without animation.

- **Animations In The Taskbar And Start Menu** Controls animations associated with jump lists, thumbnail previews, and sliding taskbar buttons. When off, no animations are used.

- **Slide Open Combo Boxes** Controls the animations associated with drop-down list boxes. When off, drop-down lists snap open.

REAL WORLD The Enable Desktop Composition option ensures that Windows creates a snapshot of each open window in memory before rendering and drawing on the desktop. When you turn this option off, Windows writes directly to the screen, which can improve performance. However, it precludes the use of glass transparency, certain animations, thumbnail previews, and other related features.

Mastering Desktop Essentials

Like a real workspace, the desktop can get cluttered. Programs that you run and folders that you open appear on the desktop in separate windows, and all these open windows can quickly make it difficult to get to the desktop itself. To quickly declutter, you can rearrange open program and folder windows by right-clicking an empty area of the taskbar and then selecting one of the following viewing options:

- **Cascade Windows** Arranges the open windows so that they overlap, with the title bar remaining visible.
- **Show Windows Stacked** Resizes the open windows and arranges them on top of each other, in one or more columns.
- **Show Windows Side by Side** Resizes the open windows and stacks them side by side.

To get to the desktop without decluttering, use the small, blank button on the far right of the taskbar. This button is called the Show Desktop button. You can:

- Temporarily make all open windows transparent by moving the pointer over the Show Desktop button. Restore the windows to their previous state by moving the pointer away.

    NOTE The feature that makes this work is called Aero Peek. Enable Aero Peek and Enable Desktop Composition must be selected on the Visual Effects tab of the Performance Options dialog box.

- Temporarily hide all open windows by clicking the Show Desktop button. Click the button again to unhide the windows and restore them to their previous state.

    TIP You don't need Aero Peek or Desktop Composition to show or hide windows in this way. Another way to hide or show open windows is to press the Windows logo key+D.

You can store files, folders, and shortcuts on the desktop for quick and easy access. Any file or folder that you drag from a Windows Explorer window to the desktop stays on the desktop. Rather than placing files or folders on the desktop, you can add a shortcut to a file or folder to the desktop by following these steps:

1. Click Start, click Computer, and then use Windows Explorer to locate the file or folder that you want to add to the desktop.

2. Right-click the file or folder. On the shortcut menu, point to Send To, and then select Desktop (Create Shortcut).

You can also add system icons to the desktop. By default, the only system icon on the desktop is the Recycle Bin. You can add or remove system icons by completing the following steps:

1. Right-click an empty area of the desktop, and then click Personalize.

2. In the left pane of the Personalization window, click Change Desktop Icons. This opens the Desktop Icon Settings dialog box, as shown in Figure 1-2.

3. Add or remove icons by selecting or clearing their related check boxes and then clicking OK to save your changes.

FIGURE 1-2 Configuring the desktop icons

Some of the desktop icons can be renamed by right-clicking the icon, clicking Rename, typing the desired name, and then pressing Enter. For example, you could rename Recycle Bin as Trash Barrel by right-clicking Recycle Bin, clicking Rename, typing **Trash Barrel**, and then pressing Enter.

If you no longer want an icon or shortcut on the desktop, right-click it, and then click Delete. When prompted, confirm the action by clicking Yes. Each icon has special options and uses:

- **Accessing computers and devices on your network** Double-clicking the Network icon opens a window where you can access the computers and devices on your network.

- **Accessing Control Panel** Double-clicking the Control Panel icon opens the Control Panel, which provides access to system configuration and management tools.

- **Accessing hard disks and devices**   Double-clicking the Computer icon opens a window from which you can access hard disk drives and devices with removable storage.

- **Accessing the System page in Control Panel**   Right-clicking the Computer icon and selecting Properties displays the System page in Control Panel.

- **Accessing Windows Explorer**   Double-clicking the folder icon opens your user profile folder in Windows Explorer.

- **Connecting to network drives**   Right-clicking the Computer icon (or the Network icon) and selecting Map Network Drive allows you to connect to shared network folders.

- **Managing your computer**   Right-clicking the Computer icon and selecting Manage opens the Computer Management console.

- **Removing deleted items**   Right-clicking the Recycle Bin icon and selecting Empty Recycle Bin permanently removes all items in the Recycle Bin.

- **Restoring deleted items**   Double-clicking the Recycle Bin icon opens the Recycle Bin, which you can use to view or restore deleted items.

REAL WORLD   Now that you know how to add items to the desktop, try this:

1. Create a custom Show Desktop button that you can place anywhere on the desktop, open Notepad.exe, type the commands below, and then save the file as Show.scf.

```
[Shell]
Command=2
IconFile=Explorer.exe,3
[Taskbar]
Command=ToggleDesktop
```

2. Double-click the related icon to hide or unhide windows.

Stretching the Desktop

Increasingly, desktop PCs and laptops support multiple display devices, allowing you to add a monitor to increase your desktop space. Not only is this a relatively inexpensive way to make your computer more useful, it can also boost your productivity.

Here's an example: You connect two monitors to your computer, or add a monitor as an additional output for your laptop. By placing the screens side by side and enabling multiple displays, you effectively stretch your desktop space and make it possible to view programs and files open on both screens at the same time. Thus, instead of having to toggle between multiple windows, you can have multiple windows open all the time—some on your primary screen and some on your secondary screen.

Typically, if a computer supports multiple displays, it has multiple display adapter connectors. For example, if a desktop PC has three display adapter connectors (two digital and one analog), it likely supports at least two monitors; if a laptop has additional display adapter connectors (digital or analog), it likely supports at least two monitors.

You can confirm the number of supported displays by checking the technical specifications for your display adapter on the manufacturer's website. To determine the type of display adapter on your computer, right-click an empty area of the desktop, and then select Screen Resolution. On the Screen Resolution page, click the Advanced Settings link. The adapter type listed for your display adapter shows the manufacturer name and model information, such as NVIDIA GeForce GT 220.

Getting a computer that supports multiple monitors to stretch the desktop across two monitors is best handled as follows:

1. With the computer shut down (and not in the sleep or hibernate state), connect the monitors to the computer, and then turn on the monitors.

2. Next, start your computer and log on.

> **TROUBLESHOOTING** The logon screen should appear on one of the monitors (although not necessarily on the one directly in front of you). If the logon screen doesn't appear, turn off both monitors in turn, and then turn the monitors back on. If a monitor has multiple modes, such as analog and digital, wait for the monitor to switch to the appropriate mode or manually configure the mode by using the monitor's configuration settings. You may need to wiggle the mouse or press keys on the keyboard to get the monitor to sense the appropriate mode.

3. Right-click an open area on the desktop, and then select Screen Resolution to open the Screen Resolution page in Control Panel, as shown in Figure 1-3.

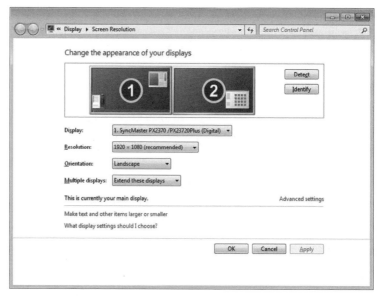

FIGURE 1-3 Identifying and orienting the displays

4. You have the choice of extending your desktop across the available display devices or duplicating the desktop on each display (as you might want to do with a laptop). Extend the desktop by clicking Extend These Displays in the Multiple Displays list and then clicking Apply. Duplicate the desktop by selecting Duplicate These Displays in the Multiple Displays list.

5. Click Detect to have Windows display the identity number of each monitor. With two monitors, the displays are numbered 1 and 2. By default, Display 1 always includes the Start menu, taskbar, and notification tray, but you can change this as discussed in the "Making the Taskbar Dance" section, later in this chapter.

6. Confirm the display order. Windows doesn't know how you've placed the monitors on your desktop. Instead, it assumes that the primary display device is the first one connected to the display adapter and the secondary display device is the second one connected. It also assumes that the second display is to the right of the first display, which allows you to move the mouse pointer to the right to go from the desktop on the first display to the desktop stretched to the second display.

7. You can tell Windows how your monitors are oriented in several ways. If Display 2 is on the left side of Display 1, click the representation of the Display 2 desktop on the Screen Resolution page, drag it to the left past the Display 1 desktop, release the mouse button, and then click Apply. The orientation should now show Display 2 on the left and Display 1 on the right; you can confirm proper configuration by clicking the Identify button. To reverse this procedure, perform the same steps, but drag to the right instead of to the left.

8. You can change the monitor that is identified as Display 1 by clicking the representation of its desktop on the Screen Resolution page, clicking Make This My Main Display, and then clicking Apply. If the monitor you've selected is already Display 1, you won't have this option.

REAL WORLD If you identify and orient the displays incorrectly, moving from the desktop on one monitor to the stretched desktop on the other monitor won't be logical. For example, if Display 2 is physically located to the right of Display 1, but you've incorrectly configured the displays, you may not be able to access the stretched desktop on Display 2 by moving the pointer to the right. Instead, you may need to move the pointer to the left, past the edge of Display 2's desktop, and vice versa.

After you've connected an additional monitor and oriented it properly, working with multiple monitors is fairly straightforward. When you stretch the desktop across two displays, the resolution setting of both displays determines the size of the desktop. If Display 1's resolution is 1920 x 1080 and Display 2's resolution is 1920 x 1080, the effective resolution is 3840 x 1080.

When you maximize windows, they fill their current display from edge to edge. You can click on windows and drag them from the desktop on one display to the stretched desktop on another display. After you click and drag a window, size it as appropriate for the way you want to use it. For many programs, Windows remembers where you've positioned a window when you close it; the next time you open the window, it appears positioned on the appropriate display, as you last worked with it. Generally, there's no special magic to make this work. However, some programs won't remember your preferred monitor, either by design or because the program isn't appropriate for multiple displays.

Any wallpaper you've selected as the background for your desktop will appear on all your displays. Whether you choose a picture position of Fill, Stretch, Fit, or Center, you see a duplicate of the background on each display. When you shuffle background images, the same shuffled image appears on each display as well.

If you want different pictures to appear on each display, you must create pictures at the appropriate resolution, store them in an appropriate folder (such as a subfolder of C:\Windows\Web\Wallpaper), select them as your desktop background, and use the Tile option of the Picture Position list. For example, if Display 1's resolution is 1920 x 1080 and Display 2's resolution is 1920 x 1080, using an art program such as Photoshop, you could combine two 1920 x 1080 images to create one 3840 x 1080 image. You would then store this image in an appropriate folder and select it as your tiled wallpaper.

You also may be wondering how your screen savers will work with multiple displays. The standard screen savers that come with Windows 7 also stretch across your displays automatically. There's no need to do anything special to make this happen.

Making the Start Menu Work for You

The Start button provides access to your computer's menu system. Clicking the Start button displays the Start menu. You also can display the Start menu by pressing the Windows logo key on your keyboard or by pressing Control+Esc.

As you probably know, and as Figure 1-4 shows, the Start menu allows you to run programs, open folders, search your computer, get help, and more. What you may not know is how to customize the Start menu so that it works the way you want it to.

> **TIP** You don't need to click in the Search box before you begin typing. Just type your search text and you'll see any matching results. The Search box also allows you to run programs. Simply type any program name in the box and press Enter to run the program. If you started a search and want to cancel it, click the blue x button to the right of the Search box or press Esc.

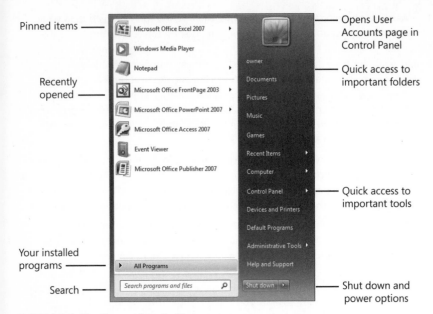

Pinned items —
Recently opened —
Your installed programs —
Search —

Opens User Accounts page in Control Panel

Quick access to important folders

Quick access to important tools

Shut down and power options

FIGURE 1-4 Getting the most from the Start menu

Customizing the Programs List

The left pane of the Start menu displays pinned programs and recently used programs. You can customize the programs list by pinning items to the Start menu and by changing the number of recently used programs to display.

Programs pinned to the Start menu are listed in the uppermost section of the programs list for quick access to your favorite programs. You can pin a program to the Start menu by following these steps:

1. Click Start, click All Programs, and then locate the program's menu entry.

2. Right-click the program's menu entry and click Pin To Start Menu.

> **REAL WORLD** Sometimes the program you want to pin is not readily accessed in the menu system. In this case, locate the application's executable file (.exe) in Windows Explorer. Right-click the file, and then select Pin To Start Menu.

By default, pinned items are listed in the order in which they are added. You can rearrange pinned items by clicking them and dragging up or down until the desired list position is reached. If you no longer want a program to be pinned to the Start menu, you can unpin it by right-clicking its entry on the Start menu and selecting Unpin From Start Menu.

On the Start menu, recently used programs are listed in the lower portion of the programs list. You can remove a program from the recently used list by right-clicking it and then selecting Remove From This List. However, this won't prevent the program from being added to the list in the future.

You can customize the recent programs list by completing the following steps:

1. Right-click the Start button, and then select Properties.

2. In the Taskbar And Start Menu Properties dialog box, click Customize on the Start Menu tab. Set the Number Of Recent Programs To Display option to the desired value.

3. By using small icons instead of large icons, you can display more programs on the list. Scroll down the list of options and clear the Use Large Icons check box.

4. Save your changes by clicking OK twice.

You can remove the recent programs list and make this extra space available for pinned programs by completing the following steps:

1. Right-click the Start button and then select Properties.

2. Clear the Store And Display Recently Opened Programs In The Start Menu check box, and then click OK.

Customizing the Important Folders and Tools List

The right pane of the Start menu provides quick access to important folders and tools, such as Documents, Pictures, Music, and Control Panel. If you upgraded from an earlier version of Windows, you'll notice that some of the familiar folders don't exist in Windows 7 or have been renamed.

In Windows 7, your documents are stored by default in personal folders under *%HomeDrive%\%HomePath%*. You can quickly open your personal folder by clicking the entry on the Start menu that shows your user name.

Opening your personal folder gives you direct access to its subfolders, such as Documents, Pictures, and Music, so you don't need related entries on the Start menu. Therefore, one way to clean up Start menu clutter is to remove these unnecessary options. If you don't play the built-in Windows games, you can remove the Games options as well.

You can remove features from the Start menu's right pane by using the Customize Start Menu dialog box. Right-click the Start button, and then select Properties. In the Taskbar And Start Menu Properties dialog box, click Customize on the Start Menu tab. In the Customize Start Menu dialog box, you can remove unwanted items in two ways:

- Clear the related check box, such as the Default Programs option.
- Set their related list option to Don't Display This Item.

While you are working with the Customize Start Menu dialog box you may want to optimize other options as well. Here are some suggestions:

- **Computer** Display this as a menu so that you can more quickly open specific drives and removable media.
- **Control Panel** If you're not a fan of Category Control Panel, display this as a menu so that you can more quickly access specific Control Panel utilities.

- **Devices And Printers** Make sure you select this option, because it is the quickest way to get to your devices and printers.
- **Default Programs** Clear this option, because you'll hardly ever use it (and if you need it, it is in Control Panel).
- **Help** Select this option, because it may come in handy in a pinch.
- **Search Programs And Control Panel** Make sure you select this option, because the Search box is the quickest way to find programs and tools.
- **System Administrative Tools** If you have appropriate permissions, select Display On The All Programs Menu And The Start Menu so you have quicker access to system tools.

Below the common folder and feature buttons in the right pane of the Start menu, you'll find your computer's Shut Down button. When you click the Shut Down options button (the arrow to the right of "Shut down"), the available options include:

- **Switch user** Switches users so another user can log on
- **Log off** Logs off the computer and ends your user session
- **Lock** Locks the computer so that a logon screen is displayed
- **Restart** Shuts down and then restarts the computer
- **Sleep** Puts the computer in sleep mode, if possible given the system configuration and state

Your computer's power configuration determines whether and how sleep mode works. When working with sleep mode, it is important to remember that the computer is still drawing power and that you should never install hardware inside the computer when it is in the sleep state.

Making the Taskbar Dance

You use the taskbar to manage your programs and open windows. The taskbar displays buttons for pinned and open items that allow you to quickly access items you've opened and start applications.

Putting the Taskbar Where You Want It

By default, the taskbar is always displayed along the bottom of the desktop on your primary monitor. If you want to move the taskbar to another location, first make sure it is not locked, as indicated by a check mark. To unlock the taskbar, right-click it and clear the Lock The Taskbar option.

After you unlock the taskbar, you can position it wherever you want by clicking on it and dragging. You can:

- Drag the taskbar to the left or right to dock it on the left or right side of the primary desktop. Drag up to dock the taskbar to the top of the primary desktop.

- Dock the taskbar to a location on another monitor. Simply drag the taskbar to the desired left, right, top, or bottom location on the stretched desktop.

After you position the taskbar where you want it, you should lock it in position. To do this, right-click an open area of the taskbar, and then select the Lock The Taskbar option. A check mark indicates that it is locked.

Customizing Taskbar Appearance

You can customize other aspects of the taskbar by using the Taskbar And Start Menu Properties dialog box, shown in Figure 1-5. To access this dialog box, right-click an open area of the taskbar, and then select Properties. Select or clear options as desired and click OK to save your changes.

FIGURE 1-5 Customizing taskbar appearance

The available options include:

- **Lock The Taskbar**   Locks the taskbar in place to prevent accidental moving or resizing. You must clear this option to move or resize the taskbar.
- **Auto-Hide The Taskbar**   Hides the taskbar when you aren't using it and displays the taskbar only when you move the cursor over it. If you clear this option, the taskbar is always displayed (although not always on top), which you may prefer, especially if you move the taskbar around a stretched desktop.

   TIP   If the taskbar is hidden and you forget where it is docked, you can quickly display the taskbar by pressing the Windows logo key.

- **Use Small Icons**   Reduces the size of taskbar buttons, allowing more buttons to fit on the taskbar. On my desktop PC, I prefer large icons, which makes them easier to click, but on my tablet PC, I prefer small icons so they take up less screen space.

- **Taskbar Location On Screen**   Sets the relative location of the taskbar on the currently targeted display. As we discussed previously, you can move the taskbar manually as well when it is unlocked.

- **Taskbar Buttons**   Specifies whether taskbar buttons are always combined, combined only when the taskbar is full, or never combined.

- **Use Aero Peek To Preview The Desktop**   Enables the peek feature with the Show Desktop button. If you clear this option, Windows doesn't temporarily hide all open windows when you move the pointer over the Show Desktop button.

See the next section for more information on combining buttons and using related options.

NOTE   Typically, you'll want to combine similar items to reduce taskbar clutter. Rather than displaying a button for each program, the taskbar groups similar buttons by default. Grouping buttons saves room on the taskbar and helps reduce the likelihood that you'll need to expand the taskbar to find the buttons for open programs.

Pinning Programs to the Taskbar

You can pin items that you work with frequently to the taskbar. Pinning an item to the taskbar creates a shortcut that allows you to quickly open a program, folder, or related window.

Pinning items is easy. If you know the name of the program you want to pin to the taskbar, click Start and start typing the program name in the Search box. When you see the program in the results list, right-click it, and then select Pin To Taskbar. From this point on, whenever you want to access the program, simply click the related icon on the taskbar.

Another way to find items to pin is to click the Start button, and then click All Programs. When you find the program you want to pin, right-click the program's menu item, and then select Pin To Taskbar.

To remove a pinned program from the taskbar, right-click its icon, and then select Unpin This Program From The Taskbar. This removes the program's button from the taskbar.

You can set the order of buttons for all opened and pinned programs. To do this, click the button on the taskbar and drag it left or right to the desired position.

When buttons are combined on the taskbar, clicking an item with multiple windows displays a thumbnail with a representation of each open window. You can now rest your pointer over a window to peek at it on the desktop (as long as the appropriate Aero features are enabled) or click a window that you want to work with to open it. For example, if you open three different folders in Windows Explorer, these items are grouped together in one taskbar button. Resting your pointer over the taskbar button displays a thumbnail with an entry for each window, allowing you to select the grouped window to open by clicking it.

Taskbar buttons make it easy to close windows as well. To close a window, whether grouped or not, move the pointer over the related taskbar button. When the thumbnail appears, move the mouse pointer to the right, and then click the close button for the window you want to close.

REAL WORLD The function of grouping and previews depends on whether your computer supports Windows Aero Glass and whether Windows Aero Glass is enabled. When you aren't using Aero Glass, moving the mouse pointer over an open program's button on the taskbar displays a menu with icons and titles for each open instance of the program. You can still switch to the window by clicking in it or close the window by moving the mouse pointer to the right and clicking the close button.

Using Flip Views and Jump Lists

Flip views and jump lists are some of the most powerful features of Windows 7. Why? They allow you to quickly get to items that you want to work with.

Display the standard flip view by pressing Alt+Tab. As shown in Figure 1-6, the flip view contains live thumbnails of all open windows, which are continuously updated to reflect their current state. You can work with a flip view in a variety of ways. Here are a few techniques:

- Press Alt+Tab, and then hold Alt to keep the flip view open.
- Press Tab while you hold the Alt key to cycle through the windows.
- Release the Alt key to bring the currently selected window to the front.
- Select a window and bring it to the front by clicking it.

FIGURE 1-6 Using the flip view

Display the 3D flip view by pressing the Windows logo key and the Tab key. As shown in Figure 1-7, the 3D flip view contains a skewed 3D view of all open windows that is continuously updated to reflect the current state. Key techniques for working with 3D flip view are as follows:

- Press the Windows logo key+Tab and hold the Windows logo key to keep the 3D flip view open.
- Press the Tab key while holding the Windows logo key to cycle through the windows.
- Release the Windows logo key to bring the currently selected window to the front.
- Select a window and bring it to the front by clicking it.

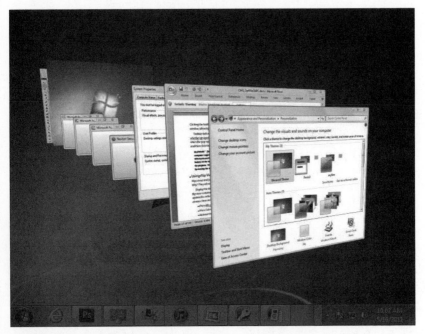

FIGURE 1-7 Using the 3D flip view

If you think flip views are cool, wait until you try jump lists. Jump lists are displayed after a short delay whenever you right-click and hover with the pointer over an item that has been pinned to the taskbar. When a program's jump list is displayed, you can select a file to open or task to perform simply by clicking it.

Most applications display recently used items or frequently used items. Some applications have enhanced jump lists that also provide quick access to tasks that you can perform with the application. The maximum number of recently or frequently used items on a program's jump list is configurable. By default, jump lists track up to 10 recent items.

You can specify the maximum number of items to display by following these steps:

1. Right-click the Start button, and then select Properties. In the Taskbar And Start Menu Properties dialog box, click Customize on the Start Menu tab.

2. In the Customize Start Menu dialog box, specify the number of recent items to display in jump lists, and then click OK twice.

Windows 7 also allows you to pin items to a program's jump list. To do this, drag an item associated with a program to the program's button pinned on the taskbar and release when the Pin To option appears. Consider the following real-world scenario:

- You want to pin Microsoft Word to the taskbar and pin important documents to its jump list. To pin Word to the taskbar, you click Start, type **Word.exe** in the Search box, right-click Word.exe in the results, and then select Pin To Taskbar.

- After pinning Word to the taskbar, you want to add important documents to its jump list. You open Windows Explorer, locate the first document, and drag the document file from the Explorer window to the Word button on the taskbar. When the Pin To Word option appears, you release the mouse button to add the first document to the jump list. You repeat this process to build your list.

Other ways to use jump lists include the following:

- If you pin Windows Explorer to the taskbar, you can add folders to its jump list. To pin Windows Explorer to the taskbar, click Start, type **Explorer.exe** in the Search box, right-click Explorer.exe in the results, and then select Pin To Taskbar. After you've pinned Windows Explorer to the taskbar, simply open Windows Explorer and locate and then drag an important folder from this window to the pinned Windows Explorer on the taskbar. When the Pin To Windows Explorer option appears, release the mouse button to add the folder to the jump list. Repeat this process to build your list.

- If you pin Control Panel to the taskbar, you can add frequently used tasks to its jump list. To pin Control Panel to the taskbar, click Start, type **Control Panel** in the Search box, right-click Control Panel in the results, and then select Pin To Taskbar. After you've pinned Control Panel to the taskbar, simply open Control Panel, locate an important task, and then drag the link for the task to the pinned Control Panel on the taskbar. When the Pin To Control Panel option appears, release the mouse button to add the task to the jump list. Repeat this process to build your list.

CHAPTER 2

Personalizing the Appearance of Windows 7

You can make Windows 7 yours by personalizing its appearance. From fine-tuning your window colors and experience level to choosing your desktop backgrounds, screen savers, sounds, mouse pointers, themes, and display settings, you can personalize Windows 7 in many ways. Navigating this maze of options can be tricky, however, especially when you want to achieve robust performance while maintaining a desired look and feel.

Many factors can affect your computer's appearance and performance, including hardware components and account controls. You achieve a balance between appearance and performance by making trade-offs when applying personalization settings, yet personalization settings largely determine the quality of your experience.

Of the many interconnected appearance and performance features, you have the most control over the following:

- Basic interfaces and account controls
- Desktop themes, screen savers, and backgrounds
- Personal account settings

In this chapter, you'll learn how to fine-tune these features while maintaining the balance between appearance and performance.

Customizing Basic Interfaces

Windows has many customizable interface features. You can customize your computer's menus, control panels, prompts, and more. This section shows you how.

Personalizing Menus

You'll often use the All Programs menu when you want to work with programs installed on your computer. The All Programs menu lists installed programs followed by a list of folders related to these and other programs on the computer.

Windows 7 manages menus differently than Windows XP and earlier versions of Windows. Windows 7 automatically sorts menus alphabetically as you add, change, or remove menus and menu items; highlights newly installed menus and programs; and opens submenus when you rest the pointer on them. Windows 7 also allows you to view shortcut menus and use drag-and-drop operations on the desktop and within menus.

You control how menus work by using the settings in the Customize Start Menu dialog box, which is accessed and optimized by following these steps:

1. Right-click the Start button, and then select Properties. This opens the Taskbar And Start Menu Properties dialog box.

2. On the Start Menu tab, click Customize to display the Customize Start Menu dialog box, shown in Figure 2-1.

3. Select Enable Context Menus And Dragging And Dropping to allow shortcut menus to be displayed and to allow dragging and dropping. Clear this option to prevent shortcut menus from being displayed and to prevent dragging and dropping.

4. Select Highlight Newly Installed Programs to highlight menus and menu items for newly installed programs. Clear this option to disable newly installed program highlighting.

5. Select Open Submenus When I Pause On Them With The Mouse Pointer to open submenus without clicking. Clear this option to require clicking a submenu to expand it and view its contents.

6. Select Sort All Programs Menu By Name to sort the menu alphabetically by name. Clear this option to show newly installed menus and menu items last.

7. Click OK to save your settings.

Personalizing Control Panel

Control Panel provides quick access to important system utilities and tasks. You can display Control Panel from any Windows Explorer view by clicking the leftmost arrow button on the Address bar and then clicking Control Panel.

You can toggle views in Control Panel by using the options on the View By list. Category view, accessed by clicking Category in the View By list, shows system utilities by category, utility name, and key tasks. All Control Panel Items view, accessed by clicking Large Icons or Small Icons in the View By list, lists all items in Control Panel alphabetically by name.

FIGURE 2-1 Configuring visual effects to optimize the desktop for the way you want to use it

In Category view, all utilities and tasks are accessed with a single click, as with options and programs on the Start Menu. You might want to configure your computer to use the more efficient single-click option to open documents, pictures, and other items as well. Configuring single-click open on all items may also help you avoid confusion as to whether you need to click or double-click something.

When you have single-click open configured, pointing to an item selects it and clicking opens it. To configure single-click open, follow these steps:

1. In Control Panel, click Appearance And Personalization.

2. Under Folder Options, click Specify Single- Or Double-Click To Open.

3. In the Folder Options dialog box, on the General tab, select Single-Click To Open An Item (Point To Select), and then click OK.

With everything set to open with one click, you might find that working with Control Panel and Windows Explorer is much more intuitive.

Fine-Tuning Control Prompts

Windows 7 has two general types of user accounts: standard and administrator. Standard users can perform any general computing tasks, such as starting programs, opening documents, and creating folders, as well as any support tasks that do not affect other users or the security of the computer. Administrators, on the other hand, have complete access to the computer and can make changes that affect other users and the security of the computer.

You can easily determine which tasks standard users and administrators can perform. You may have noticed the multicolored shield icon next to certain options in windows, wizards, and dialog boxes. This is the Permissions icon. It indicates that the related option requires administrator permissions to run.

In Windows 7, regardless of whether you are logged on as a standard user or an administrator, you see a User Account Control (UAC) prompt by default when programs try to make changes to your computer and when you try to run certain privileged applications. UAC is a collection of features designed to help protect your computer from malicious programs by improving security.

Generally, when you are logged on as a standard user, you are prompted to provide administrator credentials. On most personal or small office computers, each local computer administrator account is listed by name on the prompt, and you must click an account, type the account's password, and then click OK to proceed. If you log on to a domain, the prompt shows the logon domain and provides user name and password boxes. In this case, you must enter the name of an administrator account, type the account's password, and then click OK to proceed.

When you are logged on with an administrator account, you are prompted for consent to continue. The consent prompt works the same regardless of whether you are connected to a domain, and you must simply click OK to proceed.

The process of getting approval, prior to running an application in administrator mode and performing actions that change system-wide settings, is known as elevation. Elevation enhances security by providing notification when you are about to perform an action that could affect system settings, such as installing an application, and eliminating the ability for malicious programs to invoke administrator privileges without your knowledge and consent.

Windows 7 performs several tasks before elevating the privileges and displaying the UAC prompt, but there is just one that you need to know about: Windows switches to a secure, isolated desktop before displaying the consent prompt, which prevents other processes or applications from providing the required permissions or consent.

NOTE Only the prompt itself runs on the secure desktop. All other running programs and processes continue to run on the interactive user desktop.

Elevation, consent prompts, and the secure desktop are the key aspects of UAC that affect you and how you use your computer. To reduce the number of prompts you see, Windows 7 UAC can differentiate between changes to Windows settings and changes to the operating system made by programs and devices. Most of the time, for example, you'll only want to know when programs are trying to install themselves or make changes to the operating system; you won't want to be prompted every time you try to change Windows settings. You also can configure UAC so that the secure desktop is not used.

REAL WORLD UAC can prevent you from installing certain types of programs on your computer. Sometimes you can get around this by right-clicking the program's .exe or other installer file and selecting Run As Administrator. Keep in mind, however, that after the program is installed, it might need to always run with administrator privileges. Instead of right-clicking the program and selecting Run As Administrator every time you want to use it, make the change permanent by right-clicking the program's shortcut or installed .exe file and selecting Properties. On the Compatibility tab, in the Privilege Level section, select Run This Program As An Administrator, and then click OK.

To fine-tune UAC, follow these steps:

1. In Control Panel with Category view, click System and Security, and then under Action Center, click Change User Account Control Settings.

    TIP Alternatively, click Start, type **wscui.cpl,** and then press Enter. In Action Center, click Change User Account Control Settings.

2. On the User Account Control Settings page, shown in Figure 2-2, use the slider to choose when to be notified about changes to the computer, and then click OK to save your settings. The available options are:

    -   **Always Notify** Always notifies you when programs try to install software or make changes to the computer and when you change Windows settings. You should choose this option if your computer requires the highest security possible and you frequently install software and visit unfamiliar websites.

    -   **Default—Notify Me Only When Programs Try To Make Changes To My Computer** Notifies you only when programs try to make changes to the computer but not when you change Windows settings. You should choose this option if your computer requires high security but you want to reduce the number of notification prompts.

    -   **Notify Me Only When Programs Try To Make Changes To My Computer (Do Not Dim My Desktop)** Works the same as Default but also prevents UAC from switching to the secure desktop. You should choose this option if you work in a trusted environment with familiar applications and you do not visit unfamiliar websites. You may also want to use this option if it takes a long time for your computer to switch to the secure desktop.

    -   **Never Notify** Turns off all UAC notification prompts. You should choose this option if security is not a priority and you work in a trusted environment. If you select this option, you must restart your computer for this change to take effect.

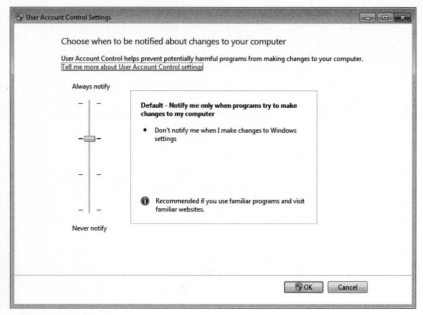

FIGURE 2-2 Optimizing UAC for the way you work

NOTE Depending on the current configuration of UAC, you may be prompted for permissions or consent. In a domain, you might not be able to manage UAC by using this technique, although you may be able to configure individual UAC features in Local Security Policy, accessible from the Administrative Tools menu: Under Security Settings, expand Local Policies, and then click Security Options.

Creating an Alternate Control Panel View

You may have heard about an alternate view for Control Panel that I've been calling the Ultimate Control Panel. To create an alternate view for Control Panel, you simply open Windows Explorer and create a new folder. Give it any name you like, followed by a period and the globally unique identifier (GUID) for the alternate Control Panel view.

The GUID is: {ED7BA470-8E54-465E-825C-99712043E01C}. For example, you could name your folder:

MyStuff.{ED7BA470-8E54-465E-825C-99712043E01C}

Or

ViewPanel.{ED7BA470-8E54-465E-825C-99712043E01C}

Or

JustCool.{ED7BA470-8E54-465E-825C-99712043E01C}

It's the GUID, not the text string, that does the magic. The GUID is a registered value in the operating system, and it identifies the alternate Control Panel view. When you create and name the folder in this way, you'll have an Ultimate Control Panel that helps you quickly perform common tasks by allowing easy navigation of many Control Panel options.

Creating a Dedicated Administrator Command Prompt

You use the command prompt to access the Windows 7 command-line interface. If you're a seasoned computer pro, you know this, and you also know that you must elevate the command prompt to perform any administrator tasks. Normally, you do this by accessing Command Prompt from the menu (on the Accessories submenu), right-clicking, and selecting Run As Administrator. You also can do this by clicking Start, typing **cmd.exe**, right-clicking Cmd in the results list, and clicking Run As Administrator. The result is the same either way: a command prompt that allows you to run tasks that require administrator privileges.

If you pinned Command Prompt to the taskbar, getting an administrator command prompt is a bit more difficult. More difficult, really? Yes, *really*. To elevate, you must right-click the pinned Command Prompt, right-click Command Prompt again in the jump list, and then select Run As Administrator.

You may be wondering if there is a workaround, and there is. Cmd.exe is stored in the *%WinDir%*\System32 folder. Locate the file, create a copy by right-clicking Cmd.exe and clicking Copy, and then paste the copy to another folder by accessing the folder, right-clicking, and then clicking Paste. It's a good idea to paste the copy into one of your personal folders, such as Documents.

Next, right-click the copy of Cmd.exe and select Properties. On the Compatibility tab, in the Privilege Level section, select Run This Program As An Administrator, and then click OK. Finally, right-click the copy of Cmd.exe again and select Pin To Start Menu or Pin To Taskbar. Now the pinned copy of Cmd.exe will always run with administrator privileges.

Optimizing Desktop Themes, Screen Savers, Backgrounds, and More

You can access personalization settings at any time by using the Personalization page in Control Panel. To access this page, simply right-click on the desktop and click Personalize. As Figure 2-3 shows, the main personalization settings control the desktop theme used by Windows 7. Desktop themes are combinations of the visual and audio elements that set the appearance of menus, icons, backgrounds, screen savers, system sounds, and mouse pointers. Whenever you switch between themes or modify certain aspects of a theme, you set the user experience level and color scheme for your computer.

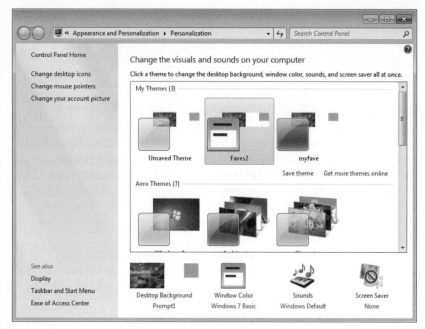

FIGURE 2-3 Customizing your computer's themes

In addition to any custom themes you create, several default themes are available. You can apply a default or saved theme by completing these steps:

1. Right-click an open area of the desktop, and then select Personalize.

2. Use the Theme list to select the theme you want to use. If you want to use a saved theme from the Microsoft website, click Get More Themes Online and select the .theme file that contains the saved theme.

Selecting and Tuning Themes

As you've seen, you can switch to any available theme by simply selecting it on the Personalization page in Control Panel. High Contrast, Windows Classic, and Windows Basic are special themes that allow you to forego the pretty stuff to improve performance, which may be necessary on an older computer.

High Contrast themes use only the most basic elements and are designed for people with vision disabilities. Windows Classic and Windows Basic themes reduce the user experience level and appearance substantially. With Windows Classic, you get the look and feel of Windows 2000 while retaining the functionality improvements in Windows 7. This means you'll have a refined Start menu and streamlined Explorer windows, both with integrated search. With Windows Basic, you add gradients and shading, and you get slightly improved performance when working with menus and windows.

When you are using Windows Classic or Windows Basic, you cannot mix colors or configure transparency settings. As a result, clicking Windows Color And Appearance opens the Appearance Settings dialog box rather than the Windows Color And Appearance page in Control Panel.

You use Windows Standard and Windows Aero themes to enhance the appearance of Windows. Windows Standard is used when Windows Aero is disabled or not otherwise available. Windows Standard supports the Windows Display Driver Model (WDDM) to enable smooth window handling, increase stability, and allow use of Windows Flip. This theme also reduces relics and slow screen refreshes when you are moving user interface elements.

Windows Aero builds on the standard experience by adding Aero Glass, transparency for all windows, live preview, and Windows Flip 3D. However, this theme is only available on a computer running Windows 7 Home Premium edition or higher (and then only when certain conditions are met).

If your computer has an older processor or doesn't have a lot of physical memory, you might want to use the Windows Classic or Windows Basic theme to improve your computer's performance. Although you won't notice much difference between the two, you can use Windows Classic to reduce the overhead associated with drawing gradients and shading.

If your computer has a newer processor and adequate physical memory, you might want to use the Windows 7 Standard or Windows Aero to improve your computer's appearance. The two themes offer very similar user experiences, but Windows Aero delivers more of the pretty stuff.

When you are using Windows 7 Standard or Windows Aero, you can use the Windows Color And Appearance page in Control Panel to change the color of windows, set color intensity, mix colors, and enable or disable transparency.

By default, Windows 7 uses the most advanced theme your computer is capable of using. To change themes, complete the following steps:

1. Right-click an open area of the desktop, and then select Personalize.
2. Select a theme to use by clicking it, and then click Window Color as necessary to fine-tune the colors your computer uses. Note that if you are using the Windows Classic or Windows Basic theme, you will not be able to mix colors or set transparency.

TIP Want more themes? Visit the themes area in the personalization gallery at *http://windows.microsoft.com/en-US/windows/downloads/personalize/themes.*

Fine-Tuning Windows Aero Colors

Windows Aero gives the user interface a highly polished, glassy look. When you use Windows Aero, you can set the glass color, intensity, and transparency by right-clicking an open area of the desktop and then selecting Personalize. On the Personalization page in Control Panel, click Window Color.

Several default colors are available, including chocolate (brown), slate (gray), ruby (red), and twilight (blue). These colors might work for you, but you can easily customize the color. Here are some tips to do this:

- To create softer or bolder colors, select a color and then slide the Color Intensity slider left or right as appropriate.

- By selecting Enable Transparency, you make it possible to see through parts of windows, menus, and dialog boxes. However, this option is resource intensive and may slow down an older computer.

- To get the exact color you want, use the color mixer options: Click Show Color Mixer, and then use the hue, saturation, and brightness sliders to get the exact color you are looking for.

NOTE The Power Saver power plan automatically disables transparency when running on batteries.

Customizing and Creating Your Own Desktop Backgrounds

If you really want to express your true self, the desktop background can help you do it. The Windows desktop can display a solid background color or a picture as its wallpaper. Windows 7 provides a starter set of background images that you can use as wallpaper.

The default wallpaper images are stored in subfolders of the *%WinDir%*\Web\ Wallpaper folder. For the most part, these images are sized for either wide-screen viewing at 1920 x 1200 or standard-screen viewing at 1900 x 1440. If you select an image at one of these sizes and your computer monitor has a different display resolution size, Windows resizes the image automatically every time the image is used.

TIP To remove the overhead associated with background resizing, you can size your background images so that they are the same size as your preferred display resolution. If you do this, however, make sure that you save the resized images to a new location and then choose this new location. Don't overwrite the existing images.

You can also create background images to use as wallpaper. To do so, simply create appropriately sized images as .bmp, .gif, .jpg, .jpeg, .dib, or .png files, and then add these files to the appropriate subfolders of the *%WinDir%*\Web\Wallpaper folder. If you do not have access to that folder, or if you would prefer to not make changes to that folder, you can also use pictures from your Pictures Library or specify a folder elsewhere.

NOTE You should optimize every background image you use. If you don't do this, you risk affecting your computer's performance because Windows will need to resize the image every time it is used.

You can set the background for the desktop by completing the following steps:

1. Right-click an open area of the desktop, and then select Personalize.

2. On the Personalization page in Control Panel, click Desktop Background. This displays the Desktop Background page, as shown in Figure 2-4.

FIGURE 2-4 Selecting a desktop background

3. Use the Picture Location menu to specify where to look for the picture you want to use, or click Browse to select a location. Your choices are:

   ■ **Pictures Library**   Displays the images in your Pictures library, which is a combination of your My Pictures folder and the Public Pictures folder by default.

   ■ **Solid Colors**   Allows you to choose one of the more than 50 pre-defined background colors or create your own background color by clicking More and then using the Color dialog box to select or mix your color.

   ■ **Top Rated Photos**   Displays the top-rated pictures in your Pictures library.

   ■ **Windows Desktop Backgrounds**   Displays the wallpaper images in the *%WinDir%*\Web\Wallpaper folder.

4. By default, when you select Windows Desktop Backgrounds, Pictures Library, or Top Rated Photos, all related images are selected automatically and the background will rotate among these images every 30 minutes. To deselect an image, clear the check box in its upper-left corner. To select multiple individual pictures, use Shift+Click. You can also select a category heading to choose all images in a category.

5. When you are using a background image, you must also use the Picture
    Position option to select a display option for the background. The
    positioning options are:

    - **Center**   Centers the image on the desktop background. Any area
      that the image doesn't fill uses the current desktop background color.
      Click Change Background Color to set the background color for the area
      the image doesn't fill.

    - **Fill**   Fills the desktop background with the image. Generally, the fill is
      accomplished by zooming in, which may result in the sides of the image
      being cropped.

    - **Fit**   Fits the image to the desktop background. Because current
      proportions are maintained in most cases, this is a good option for photos
      and large images that you want to see without stretching or expanding.

    - **Stretch**   Stretches the image to fill the desktop background. The
      proportions are maintained as closely as possible, and then the height is
      stretched to fill any remaining gaps.

    - **Tile**   Repeats the image so that it covers the entire screen. This is a good
      option for small images and icons (and also to get a single image to fill
      two screens, as discussed in Chapter 1, "Customizing the Windows 7
      Interface").

6. If you are using multiple background images, use the Change Picture Every
    list to specify how often Windows should change the background image,
    such as every 5 minutes or every 1 hour. Normally, Windows cycles through
    the images in order. To cycle through the images randomly, select the Shuffle
    check box.

7. When you are finished updating the background, click Save Changes.

REAL WORLD   When you choose Windows Desktop Backgrounds as the picture
location, you see several categories of pictures, such as Architecture, Landscapes,
and Nature. These categories are based on the names of the subfolders in the
%WinDir%\Web\Wallpaper folder; you can create additional categories by creating
new subfolders and adding backgrounds as appropriate to these folders.

PRO TIP   Want to change the background on the logon screen? You can do it, but it's
a bit tricky. The logon screen background is configurable by computer manufacturers.
If one was created for your computer, it is stored in the *%WinDir%*\System32\OOBE\
Info\Backgrounds folder as background.bmp with default dimensions of 1024 x 768.

TIP   Want more backgrounds? Visit the background page in the personalization
gallery at *http://windows.microsoft.com/en-US/windows/downloads/personalize/
wallpaper-desktop-background.*

Choosing and Configuring Your Screen Saver

You also can express yourself by using screen savers. Screen savers can be configured to turn on when a computer has been idle for a specified period. Screen savers were originally designed to prevent image burn-in by displaying a continually changing image. With today's monitors, burn-in is not really a problem, but screen savers are still around because they offer a different benefit today: the ability to password-lock your computer automatically when the screen saver turns on.

Windows 7 performs many housekeeping tasks in the background when your computer is idle, such as creating indexes, defragmenting hard disks, creating whole computer backups, and setting system restore points. Although you can install that wild screen saver you've been eyeing, you may want to ensure that generating its images doesn't use resources needed to efficiently perform these background tasks during idle time.

You can configure your screen saver by performing the following steps:

1. Right-click an open area of the desktop, and then select Personalize.

2. Click Screen Saver to open the Screen Saver Settings dialog box.

3. Use the Screen Saver list, shown in Figure 2-5, to select a screen saver. Although you can install additional screen savers, the standard options are as follows:

   - **(None)** Turns off the screen saver.

   - **3D Text** Displays the system time or custom text as a 3D message against a black background. (Uses the file *%WinDir%*\System32\ SsText3d.scr)

   - **Blank** Displays a blank screen (a black background with no text or images). (Uses the file *%WinDir%*\System32\Scrnsave.scr)

   - **Bubbles** Displays multicolored bubbles floating across your desktop while the open windows and documents on the desktop remain visible. (Uses the file *%WinDir%*\System32\Bubbles.scr)

   - **Mystify** Displays arcing bands of lines in various geometric patterns against a black background. (Uses the file *%WinDir%*\System32\ Mystify.scr)

   - **Photos** Displays photos and videos from a selected folder as a slideshow. Make sure you know what images will be shown before you set this up to avoid potential embarrassment. (Uses the file *%WinDir%*\System32\PhotoScreensaver.scr)

   - **Ribbons** Displays ribbons of various thicknesses and changing lines against a black background. (Uses the file *%WinDir%*\System32\ Ribbons.scr)

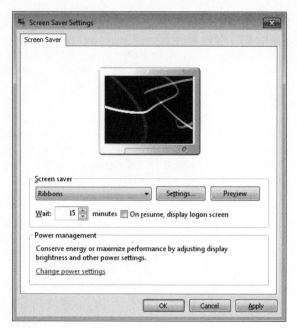

FIGURE 2-5 Choosing a screen saver

4. Password-protect the screen saver by selecting On Resume, Display Logon Screen. Clear this option only if you do not want to use password protection.

5. Use the Wait control to specify how long the computer must be idle before the screen saver is activated. At home, a reasonable value is between 10 and 15 minutes. At the office, you might want to set this to between 5 and 7 minutes. In many offices, the Wait setting is set by corporate policy and cannot be changed.

6. Click OK.

The Photos and 3D Text screen savers have additional options (as will just about any custom screen savers you install). The Photos screen saver displays a slideshow of photos, such as your portfolio or family pictures.

To customize the Photos screen saver, follow these steps:

1. In the Screen Saver Settings dialog box, select Photos, and then click Settings to display the Photos Screen Saver dialog box shown in Figure 2-6.

2. By default, this screen saver displays the images in your Pictures library, which is a combination of your My Pictures folder and the Public Pictures folder. To use photos from a different folder, click Browse, and then select the folder you want to use.

3. Use Slide Show Speed list to set the speed of the slideshow. The options are Slow, Medium, and Fast.

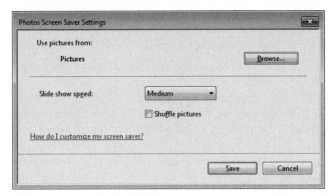

FIGURE 2-6 Fine-tuning the photos screen saver

4. Photos are displayed in alphanumeric order by default. If you want to shuffle the photos and display them in random order, select the Shuffle Pictures check box.

5. Click Save, and then click OK.

TIP If you've installed Windows Live Essentials and selected Windows Live Photo Gallery, you'll also have the option to use the Windows Live Photo Gallery screen saver. This screen saver functions much like the Photos screen saver, but it includes additional options such as a transitions choice and the ability to specify photos by tag or rating.

To customize the 3D Text screen saver, follow these steps:

1. In the Screen Saver Settings dialog box, select 3D Text, and then click Settings to display the 3D Text Settings dialog box shown in Figure 2-7.

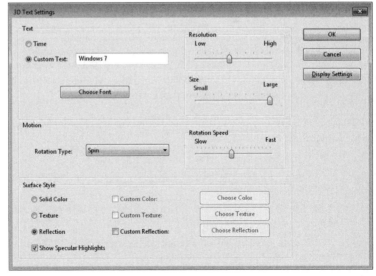

FIGURE 2-7 Fine-tuning the 3D text screen saver

2. Display the current time or a custom message as 3D text. To display the current time as 3D text, select Time. To display a custom message as 3D text, select Custom Text and type your message.

3. Click Choose Font, and then use the Font dialog box to set the font for the 3D text. The default font is Tahoma.

4. Use the Resolution slider to control the display resolution of the text and the Size slider to control the size of the text. The higher the resolution and larger the text, the more processing power required to draw and move the message.

5. Use the Rotation Speed slider to control the speed at which the text moves and rotates on the screen. The faster the rotation, the more processing power required to draw and move the message.

6. Use the Rotation Type list to select the type of rotation to use, such as tumble or spin. Set the rotation type to None to turn off rotation and reduce the amount of processing power required to draw and move the message.

7. Use the Surface Style options to configure the way the 3D text looks. For example, Solid Color displays the text in a solid color. Click Custom Color and then click Choose Color to display the Color dialog box. Choose the color to use, and then click OK.

8. Click OK twice to save your settings.

Configuring and Creating Your System Sounds

A sound scheme is a set of sounds that you use together. Windows 7 plays sounds in response to a wide variety of events, such as when you log on, when you open or close programs, and when you log off. Programs you install can have their own sounds as well. You manage all of these sounds collectively by using sound schemes.

> **TIP** Want your computer to play a snippet from a particular song when you log on or log off? You can do this! When you're configuring sounds for your computer, Windows Logon and Windows Logoff are listed under program events. Simply use any sound editor to create a .wav snippet from the original song files and configure the resulting .wav files for each related event in the Program Events list.

You can configure your system to use an existing sound scheme by completing the following steps:

1. Right-click an open area of the desktop, and then click Personalize.

2. Click Sounds to display the Sound dialog box with the Sounds tab selected, as shown in Figure 2-8.

3. Use the Sound Scheme list to choose the sound scheme to use. Windows 7 has two standard sound schemes:

   ▪ No Sounds, which turns off all program sounds except the Windows Startup sound played when you log on.

FIGURE 2-8 Selecting your system sounds

- Windows Default, which is configured to use the standard Windows sounds.

NOTE Other sound schemes available typically depend on the edition of Windows 7 installed on your computer and the extras you've installed. Some of the available sound schemes you might see include Afternoon, Calligraphy, Characters, Cityscape, Delta, Festival, Garden, Heritage, Landscape, Quirky, Raga, Savanna, and Sonata.

4. In the Program Events list, sounds are organized according to the program to which they relate and the related event that triggers the sound. To preview a sound for a particular event, select the event in the program list and then click Test.

5. To change the sound for an event, select the event in the Program Events list and then use the Sounds list to choose an available sound. You can also click Browse to select other sounds available on the system. The sound files must be in Microsoft .wav format.

6. If you changed the default sounds for a scheme and want to save the changes, click Save As, type a name for the scheme in the field provided, and then click OK.

7. Save your sound settings by clicking OK.

TIP Want to access the Sound dialog box directly? Click Start, type **Mmsys.cpl**, and then press Enter.

Customizing Your Mouse Pointers

A pointer scheme is a set of mouse pointers that you use together. The three types of mouse pointers you see the most are the Normal Select pointer, the Text Select pointer, and the Link Select pointer. You can configure the appearance of these and other types of mouse pointers and manage them collectively by using pointer schemes.

The available pointer schemes include:

- **(None)**   This doesn't turn mouse pointers off. Instead, it uses nondescript pointers.
- **Windows Aero**   The standard pointers used with Windows Aero settings. Also comes in large and extra-large options.
- **Windows Black**   Inverts the pointer colors so that black backgrounds are used instead of white backgrounds. Also comes in large and extra-large options.
- **Windows Standard**   The standard pointers used with Windows Standard settings. Also comes in large and extra-large options.

You can configure your system to use an existing pointer scheme by completing the following steps:

1. Right-click an open area of the desktop, and then select Personalize.
2. In the left pane, click Change Mouse Pointers to display the Mouse Properties dialog box with the Pointers tab selected, as shown in Figure 2-9.

FIGURE 2-9 Selecting your mouse pointers

3. Use the Scheme list to choose the pointer scheme to use.

4. In the Customize list, pointers are organized according to their type. To change a pointer, select the pointer and then click Browse. This opens the Browse dialog box with the Cursors folder selected. Choose the cursor pointer to use, and then click Open.

5. If you changed the default pointers for a scheme and want to save the changes, click Save As, type a name for the scheme in the field provided, and then click OK.

6. Save your pointer settings by clicking OK.

TIP To manage mouse settings as well as pointers, click Start, type **Main.cpl,** and then press Enter. You can now configure mouse buttons, pointers, scrolling, and more.

Saving Your Custom Themes and Creating Theme Packs

So far you have tuned and tweaked window colors, backgrounds, sounds, pointers, and screen savers. Now you'll want to save your settings as a unified theme so you can be sure that you can use it again and again. To do this, follow these steps:

1. Right-click an open area of the desktop, and then select Personalize.

2. On the Personalization page, under the My Themes heading, you'll see Unsaved Theme. Right-click this theme, and then select Save Theme.

3. In the Save Theme As dialog box, enter a name for your custom theme and then click Save. Theme definition files end with the .theme file extension.

4. Unless deleted in the future, the custom theme will appear as a My Themes option. You'll then be able to load the theme simply by clicking it.

A theme you save in this way will only be available to you. That's because the theme is saved in your user profile (%UserProfile%\AppData\Local\Microsoft\Windows\Themes). If you want to be able to share the theme with others, you must create a theme pack by following these steps:

1. Right-click an open area of the desktop, and then select Personalize.

2. On the Personalization page, under the My Themes heading, you'll see Unsaved Theme. Right-click this theme, and then select Save Theme For Sharing.

3. In the Save Theme Pack As dialog box, enter a name for your custom theme pack and then click Save. Theme pack definition files end with the .themepack file extension and are saved in Libraries\Documents by default. Saved theme packs can be several megabytes in size.

4. Copy the theme pack to a folder accessible to the person you are sharing with. Have the person double-click the theme pack file to load it as a theme and save it to his or her own My Themes list.

TIP You might be wondering how you delete a custom theme that you no longer want. To do this, select a different theme, right-click the theme you no longer want in the My Themes list, and then click Delete Theme.

Customizing Your Displays

In Chapter 1, you learned how to configure multiple displays. Now let's take a closer look at customizing individual display settings.

Windows 7 automatically optimizes display settings for each of your monitors by selecting a screen resolution, refresh rate, and color bitness that seem most appropriate based on its testing. Normally, the settings Windows selects work well, but they might not be the optimal settings for your computer.

You can adjust display settings by completing the following steps:

1. Right-click an open area of the desktop, and then select Screen Resolution. Display 1 is selected by default. If you want to configure the second monitor, click 2 to select it.

2. Use the Resolution list to set the display size, such as 1920 × 1200 pixels. Optionally, use the Orientation list to specify an alternate orientation for a monitor, such as portrait. The default orientation is landscape.

3. Click Advanced Settings. Set the color quality or refresh rate using one of the following options:

   ■ On the Adapter tab, click List All Modes. The List All Modes dialog box shows the color qualities and refresh rates supported by the selected monitor. Click OK.

   ■ On the Monitor tab, use the Screen Refresh Rate list to set the desired refresh rate. Use the Colors list to select a color quality, such as True Color (32 bit).

4. Click OK twice to save your settings.

TIP Windows 7 will display refresh rates that exceed the capabilities of the monitor and graphics card if you clear the Hide Modes That This Monitor Cannot Display check box. Select these additional hidden modes only when you know for sure that your monitor and graphics card support a particular mode, such as when you are using a generic driver but actually have a more powerful graphics card installed. Remember that running the computer at a higher refresh rate than it supports can damage the monitor and video adapter. For certain displays, this check box may be disabled.

If the monitor or graphics card shown in the display Properties dialog box does not match the one you are using, you should visit your computer, monitor, or graphics card manufacturer's website and obtain the proper driver. Typically, you can do this by accessing the manufacturer's support page and entering the model of your computer, monitor, or graphics card.

Most manufacturers maintain drivers for several years and provide updates for these drivers as they become available. Typically, the update is delivered in a zipped file containing the drivers you need and an executable installer. To extract the files from a ZIP, right-click the .zip file and select Extract All. After you select a destination folder, click Extract.

You install monitor drives and graphics card drivers using separate procedures. To specify the monitor driver to use, follow these steps:

1. Right-click an open area of the desktop, and then select Screen Resolution. Display 1 is selected by default. Click 2 to configure settings for the second monitor.

2. Click Advanced Settings. On the Monitor tab, click Properties.

3. On the Driver tab, click Update Driver to start the Update Driver Software wizard. Click Browse My Computer For Driver Software.

4. Select a search location by clicking Browse, using the Browse For Folder dialog box to select the start folder for the search, and then clicking OK. Windows 7 searches all subfolders of the selected folder automatically, and you can select the drive root path, such as C, to search an entire drive.

5. Click Next. Click Close when the driver installation is completed.

Typically, graphics drivers are installed using an executable installer. Run the installer and reboot if the installer asks you to do so. Otherwise, manually specify the graphics card driver to use by following these steps:

1. Right-click an open area of the desktop, and then select Screen Resolution. Display 1 is selected by default. Click 2 to configure settings for the second monitor.

2. Click Advanced Settings. On the Adapter tab, click Properties.

3. On the Driver tab, click Update Driver to start the Update Driver Software wizard. Click Browse My Computer For Driver Software.

4. Select a search location by clicking Browse, using the Browse For Folder dialog box to select the start folder for the search, and then clicking OK. Windows 7 searches all subfolders of the selected folder automatically, and you can select the drive root path, such as C, to search an entire drive.

5. Click Next. Click Close when the driver installation is completed.

Color profiles allow you to get truer colors for specific uses. For example, you may need to more accurately match on-screen colors to print colors, and a color profile designed for this purpose can help you do that. After you obtain the color profile, you must install it on each monitor separately by following these steps:

1. Right-click an open area of the desktop, and then select Screen Resolution. Display 1 is selected by default. Click 2 to configure settings for the second monitor.

2. Click Advanced Settings. On the Color Management tab, click Color Management.

3. In the Color Management dialog box, select the All Profiles tab to get information about currently installed color profiles. Click Add.

4. In the Install Profile dialog box, find the color profile you want to use and then click Add.

5. In the Color Management dialog box, select the Devices tab. Click the new profile, and then select Set As Default Profile.

TIP Want to get to the Color Management dialog box directly? Click Start, type **Colorcpl.exe,** and then press Enter. When you access color management in this way, be sure to use the Device list to choose the display you want to work with.

REAL WORLD If you don't have a color profile and still would like the benefits of one, use the Display Color Calibration tool to fine-tune display colors to your liking. You can access this tool by clicking Start, typing **Dccw.exe,** and pressing Enter.

As discussed in Chapter 1, if multiple monitors are connected to your computer, you can designate one monitor as the primary and the other as the secondary monitor. You can also extend the desktop onto your second monitor. After you've configured your monitors, you'll find that pressing the Windows logo key+P is a convenient way to quickly change the monitor configuration. After pressing the Windows log key+P, you can:

- Select Computer Only to use only the main computer monitor or the built-in screen on a laptop.

- Select Duplicate to display the main computer monitor or the built-in screen on a laptop on a second monitor.

- Select Extend to extend the display across two monitors.

- Select Projector Only to display only on an external monitor or projector.

Customizing and Safeguarding Your User Account

Your user account has many properties, including a password, a picture, an account name, and an account type designation. You can manage the properties associated with your user account, except in a domain, as long as you have an administrator account or the user name and password of an administrator account.

REAL WORLD Throughout this section, we'll be working with the User Accounts page in Control Panel. You can access this page in several ways. In Category Control Panel view, you access this page by clicking User Accounts And Family Safety and then clicking User Accounts. In Small Icons or Large Icons Control Panel view, you access this page simply by clicking User Accounts.

If you pinned Control Panel to the taskbar as discussed in Chapter 1, drag the green User Accounts link to the pinned Control Panel on the taskbar. When the Pin To Control Panel option appears, release the mouse button to add User Accounts to the jump list. You'll then be able to right-click Control Panel on the task bar and click User Accounts to directly and quickly access User Accounts.

Changing Your Account Name

You can safely change your user account name at any time without worrying that this will cause problems with your access permissions or privileges. When you change your name, Windows automatically updates related settings for you.

REAL WORLD Your account name is simply a friendly name tied to the unique numeric account identifier that Windows uses to represent your account internally. When you change your account name, Windows updates this friendly name. The identifier itself is unchanged.

You can change your account name by following these steps:

1. Access the User Accounts page by clicking Start and then clicking the picture for your account on the Start menu.

2. On the User Accounts page in Control Panel, click Change Your Account Name.

3. On the Change Your Name page, type the new name for your account, and then click Change Name.

If your computer is joined to a domain, the steps to change account properties will be slightly different.

NOTE Your computer's friendly name is mapped to a unique numeric identifier as well. You can view or change the computer's friendly name in Control Panel. Click Start, type **SystemPropertiesComputerName,** and then press Enter. Click Change in the dialog box provided. Enter a new computer name, and then click OK twice.

Changing and Creating Account Pictures

Your account picture is displayed on the logon screen and on the Start menu. Microsoft provides several default pictures for accounts, but you can use any picture you want.

When you use a picture other than a default picture provided by Microsoft, Windows 7 automatically optimizes the picture and saves the optimized copy as part of your personal Contact entry in Windows Contacts. Although it may seem strange to save the picture as part of your personal .contact file, doing so is a quick and easy shortcut for the operating system. Most pictures are optimized to a file size of 50 KB or less—even high-resolution pictures.

To change your account picture, follow these steps:

1. Access the User Accounts page by clicking Start and then clicking the picture for your account on the Start menu.

2. Click Change Your Picture. On the Change Your Picture page, shown in Figure 2-10, click the picture you want to use, or click Browse For More Pictures to select any BMP, GIF, JPEG, PNG, DIB, or RLE picture to use.

3. Click Change Picture. Your picture appears on the Start menu and the logon screen.

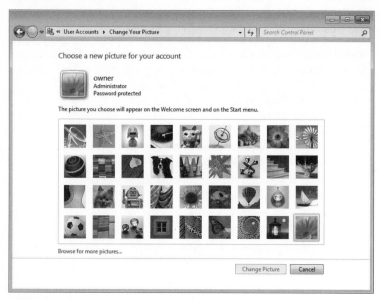

FIGURE 2-10 Choosing a picture for your user account

Changing Your Account Type

User accounts are either standard user accounts with limited privileges or administrator user accounts with full privileges. As a safety precaution, you might want to use a standard account for web browsing and other online activities and the administrator account only when you need to manage or maintain your computer.

It's common for computers to have multiple users, resulting in *several* user accounts created on it, and at least one of these must be an administrator account. If you are logged on with a standard user account, you can change the account type to Administrator. If you are logged on with an administrator account, you can change the account type to Standard User (as long as it's not the last administrator account on the computer).

REAL WORLD Ideally, you should create at least two administrator accounts on your computer—with passwords. If you forget the password for one account, you can simply log on with the other account and use the User Accounts options in Control Panel to change your password. But only do this if you've truly lost your password and cannot recover it as described later. Why? When you change an account password via another account, you'll lose all EFS-encrypted files, personal certificates, and stored passwords for both websites and network resources.

You can change the account type by following these steps:

1. Access the User Accounts page by clicking Start and then clicking the picture for your account on the Start menu.
2. Click Change Your Account Type. On the Change Your Account Type page, select either Standard User or Administrator and click Change Account Type.

Creating, Storing, and Restoring Your Account Password

Protect your computer by creating a password for your user account. If your account doesn't currently have a password, you can create a password by completing the following steps:

1. Access the User Accounts page by clicking Start and then clicking the picture for your account on the Start menu.
2. Click Create A Password For Your Account. Type a password, confirm it, and then type a unique password hint.
3. Click Create Password.

NOTE The password hint is a word or phrase that can help you remember the password if you forget it. This hint is visible to anyone who uses your computer, so be careful what you use.

Periodically, you should change your password. This makes it more difficult for someone to gain access to your computer. You can change your password by completing the following steps:

1. Access the User Accounts page by clicking Start and then clicking the picture for your account on the Start menu.
2. Click Change Your Password. Type your current password in the first text box provided.
3. Type your new password in the second text box, and confirm your new password by retyping it in the third text box.
4. Type a unique password hint, and then click Change Password.

You can store your password in a secure, encrypted file on a USB flash drive, and then use this file to recover your password if you forget it. You can store your password for recovery by completing these steps:

1. Make sure the USB flash drive is inserted before you begin. If you insert the device after starting the process, it won't be listed automatically. Click Back, and then click Next to update the list to include the device you just inserted.
2. Press Ctrl+Alt+Delete, and then click the Change A Password option.
3. Click Create A Password Reset Disk to start the Forgotten Password Wizard. Read the introductory message, and then click Next. Select your flash drive or memory card on the drive list. Click Next.
4. Type your current password in the text box provided, and then click Next.

5. After the wizard creates the password reset key, click Next, and then click Finish. Remove and store your USB flash drive in a safe location. Anyone who has this drive can use it to access your account.

Recovering your password after you've made these preparations is fairly easy. To access your password hint or recover your password, complete the following steps:

1. On the logon screen, click your user name to display the Password prompt.

2. Click the button to the right of the password text box without entering a password.

3. When you click OK, the password hint for your account is displayed on the logon screen.

4. Type your password and click the logon button. If you log on successfully, skip the remaining steps. Otherwise, click OK and continue with password recovery.

5. On the logon screen, click Reset Password. When the Reset Password Wizard starts, click Next.

6. Insert the USB flash drive containing your password recovery file, and then click Next.

7. Type a new password in the first text box. Confirm your new password by retyping it in the second text box.

8. Type a new password hint in the third text box, and then click Next to log on with your new password.

CHAPTER 3

Customizing Boot, Startup, and Power Options

I f you really want to know how a car works, you need to open the hood and take a look at the parts that make it go. The same is true for your computer. Open the case of your computer and you'll see the actual parts that make your computer go: hard disk drives and disk controllers, central processing units, memory modules, and more, all connected via wires or circuitry to your computer's motherboard.

But attaching a myriad of devices with wires and circuitry to a motherboard isn't what makes them work together. What makes them work together is your computer's firmware interface, which acts as the intermediary among devices; their internal code, if present; and higher-level processes.

Customizing Your Computer's Firmware Interface

The way a firmware interface operates and the tasks it performs depend on the type of firmware interface and the type of central processing unit (CPU). Most computers built today have CPUs based on 32-bit x86 architecture or 64-bit extensions to this architecture referred to as x64 architecture.

Generally, computers with 32-bit x86 architectures use the Basic Input Output System (BIOS) as their firmware interface, whereas computers with x64-based architectures use Unified Extensible Firmware Interface (UEFI), which is wrapped around BIOS (but can also be wrapped around standard Extensible Firmware Interface, or EFI). For our purposes, a computer that uses UEFI wrapped around BIOS is BIOS-based, as is a computer that uses BIOS by itself.

CAUTION Only change firmware interface settings when you fully understand the possible repercussions of doing so. Improperly configuring a computer's firmware interface may prevent it from booting and starting the operating system. You should document every change you make to your computer's firmware interface in a notebook. If you get into trouble, you may be able to restore your computer's factory default settings by using an option in the firmware interface. Keep in mind, however, that the factory default settings may not be the same as the settings configured when your computer was delivered to you.

Getting to Know Your Computer's Firmware Interface

Firmware interfaces know little about the operating system your computer is running. Windows XP and earlier versions of Windows used Boot.ini to initialize the startup environment and Ntldr to load the operating system. Windows 7 initializes itself by loading a pre-operating system boot environment prior to loading the operating system. This boot environment helps your computer validate the integrity of startup processes and the operating system itself before actually running the operating system.

The boot environment also acts as an abstraction layer between the firmware interface and the operating system. By abstracting the underlying interfaces, the boot environment allows Windows 7 to work with BIOS, EFI, and any other underlying interface framework in the same way.

Your computer's firmware interface manages the preboot data flow between the operating system and attached devices. When the firmware interface initializes your computer, it first determines whether all attached devices are available and functioning, and then it activates all the hardware required by the computer to boot, including:

- Graphics and audio controllers
- Internal drives and controllers
- Internal expansion cards
- Motherboard chipsets
- Processors and processor caches
- System memory

After the firmware interface completes this process, it transfers control of the computer to the operating system. The firmware interface implementation determines what happens next. With BIOS-based computers running Windows Vista and Windows 7, Windows Boot Manager and Windows Boot Loader are used to boot into the operating system. Windows Boot Manager initializes the operating system by starting the Windows Boot Loader, which in turn starts the operating system using information in the boot configuration data (BCD) store.

Entries in the BCD store identify the boot manager to use during startup and the specific boot applications available on your computer. Windows Boot Manager controls the boot experience and lets you choose the boot application to run. Boot applications load a specific operating system or operating system version. For example, Windows 7 is loaded by a Windows Boot Loader application.

Through BCD parameters, you can add options that control the way the operating system starts, the way computer components are used, and the way operating system features are used.

NOTE With UEFI, UEFI boot services provide an abstraction layer wrapped around BIOS or EFI. A computer with BIOS in its underlying architecture uses a BIOS-based approach to booting into the operating system. A computer with EFI in its underlying architecture uses an EFI-based approach to booting into the operating system.

Accessing and Setting Your Computer's Firmware Interface

When you turn on most computers, you access the firmware interface by pressing the button shown for Setup in the initial display. For example, you might press F2 during the first few seconds of startup to enter the firmware interface. Firmware interfaces have control options that allow you to adjust the functionality of hardware. You can use these controls to perform basic tasks, including:

- Accessing firmware event logs for troubleshooting information
- Adjusting display brightness (on laptop computers)
- Adjusting the hard disk noise level
- Adjusting the number of cores the processor uses and their speed
- Changing the boot sequence for devices
- Changing the motherboard clock's date and time
- Obtaining configuration information for memory, processors, and more
- Restoring the firmware interface to its default (factory) configuration
- Turning on or off modular add-on devices

While you are working with the firmware interface, you may also be able to create supervisor, user, and general passwords that are not accessible from the operating system. When a supervisor password is set, you must provide the password before you can modify the firmware configuration. When a user password is set, you must enter the password during startup before the computer will load the operating system. If you forget these passwords, you might not be able to operate the computer or change firmware settings until you clear the forgotten passwords, which generally also clears any customization you have made to the firmware interface.

The way the firmware interface works depends on the computer you are working with, the type of firmware interface, and the version of the firmware interface. Desktop computers typically have more firmware configuration options than portable computers do.

Most firmware interfaces have several menu pages that provide information and controls. Two important controls you'll see are network boot and boot order. When network booting is enabled, the computer boots from the network. This is something you might want at the office, but you generally don't want this enabled at home. Boot order sets the priority order for your computer's bootable devices. Your computer tries to start the operating system using the highest-priority device first. If this fails, your computer tries the device with the second-highest priority, and so on. Generally, you'll want your computer to look to its primary removable media device first, and its primary hard drive next, before looking to other bootable devices.

Because configuring boot options in firmware isn't necessarily intuitive, I'll provide two examples using computers from different manufacturers. On a Dell desktop computer that I have, you manage boot settings on the Boot Sequence submenu under System in the firmware interface. The boot order is listed as follows (based on the device present in my computer):

1. Onboard or USB CD-ROM Drive
2. Onboard SATA Hard Drive
3. Onboard or USB Floppy Drive (not present)
4. Onboard IDE Hard Drive (not present)
5. Add-in Hard Drive (not present)
6. USB Device (not present)
7. Add-in Hard Drive (not present)

In this example, internal devices are listed as "Onboard." Because you generally want the computer to check its primary CD-ROM or DVD-ROM drive for bootable media first and then check its primary hard drive, the computer's primary CD-ROM drive has the highest boot order, and the computer's primary hard drive is listed with the second-highest boot order.

Several options are available for navigating the list. You can use the Up and Down arrow keys to select a device, and then press the U or D key to move the device up or down in the boot order list. You can press the Spacebar to exclude or include a device from the boot list. Press Delete to permanently delete the device if it is not physically present and you no longer want it in the list.

Other important menus in the interface include the following:

- Under Drives in the firmware interface, submenus allow you to enable, disable, and configure drives. Diskette Drive configures floppy drives. Drive 0: SATA-0 enables or disables this specific device. Drive 1: SATA-1 enables or disables this device. SATA Operation sets the hardware RAID configuration.

- Under Onboard Devices, you can use the options on the USB Controller submenu to enable or disable booting from USB storage devices.

For comparison, on an HP laptop of mine, the boot settings are found on the Boot Order and Boot Options submenus on the firmware interface's System Configuration page. On the Boot Order submenu, the boot order is listed as follows:

1. USB Floppy
2. ATAPI CD/DVD ROM Drive
3. Notebook Hard Drive
4. USB Diskette on Key
5. USB Hard Drive
6. Network Adapter

On this computer, you use the Up and Down arrow keys to select a device, and then press F5 or F6 to move the device up or down in the list. The computer distinguishes between USB flash keys (referred to as USB diskettes on keys) and USB drives (referred to as USB hard drives). However, you won't really see a difference between the two.

The Boot Options submenu has these options:

- **F10 and F12 Delay (sec)**   Specifies the amount of time you have to press F10 or F12 before startup begins.

- **CD-ROM Boot**   Controls whether CD-ROM boot during startup is enabled or disabled.

- **Floppy Boot**   Controls whether floppy boot during startup is enabled or disabled.

- **Internal Network Adapter Boot**   Controls whether network boot during startup is enabled or disabled.

Here, the main options for navigating the list are the Up and Down arrow keys. You use these keys to select an option, and then press Enter to view and set the option.

Every firmware interface has an Exit option. The Exit page allows you to exit the firmware interface and resume startup of the computer. Pay particular attention to the related options. Generally, you can either exit the firmware interface and discard your changes or exit the firmware interface and save your changes. Save only when you are certain that you've correctly modified the firmware interface. Incorrectly configuring the firmware interface can make your computer unbootable.

Desktop computers can have a dizzying array of options and suboptions. And because there are few standards and conventions among firmware interface manufacturers, firmware interface options with similar purposes can have very different labels. In Appendix A Table A-1 shows a composite of options I've encountered in my workplace. When you are working with a desktop computer, you'll likely find options that serve similar purposes, and you may want to customize these options for the way in which you want your computer to work.

REAL WORLD Your computer's firmware interface is updatable, and you may need to update the firmware to resolve problems or improve efficiency. However, if you are not experiencing problems on a computer and are not aware of any additional functionality in the firmware interface that you need, you might not need to update a computer to the latest version of the firmware interface. Remember that an improper update can harm the computer and prevent it from starting.

Tracking and Configuring Power On and Resume

Knowing the sequence of events for a cold start of a computer from power on through log on can help you understand exactly how your computer works. When you press the power button to turn on your computer, many events happen in the background:

1. The firmware interface performs a Power On Self Test (POST) to preliminarily configure the computer and then performs setup to initialize the computer.

    NOTE A cold start is the initial power on of a computer. The sequence of events varies if the computer is resuming from sleep, standby, or hibernation, as well as if you are starting an operating system other than Windows or a Windows operating system other than Windows Vista, Windows 7, or Windows Server 2008.

2. The firmware interface passes control to the operating system loader, which in this case is the boot manager. The boot manager starts the boot loader. The boot loader uses the firmware interface's boot services to complete operating system boot and then load the operating system.

3. The operating system loads, which involves the following:

    a. Loading (but not running) the operating system kernel, Ntoskrnl.exe

    b. Loading (but not running) the hardware abstraction layer (HAL), Hal.dll

    c. Loading the HKEY_LOCAL_MACHINE\SYSTEM registry hive into memory (from *%SystemRoot%*\System32\Config\System)

    d. Scanning the HKEY_LOCAL_MACHINE\SYSTEM\Services key for device drivers and then loading (but not initializing) the drivers that are configured for the boot class into memory

    NOTE In this context, drivers are also services. This means that both device drivers and system services are prepared.

    e. Enabling memory paging

4. The boot loader passes control to the operating system kernel. The kernel and the HAL initialize the Windows executive, which in turn processes the configuration information stored in the HKEY_LOCAL_MACHINE\SYSTEM\CurrentControlSet hive and then starts device drivers and system services.

5. The kernel starts the Session Manager (Smss.exe). The session manager:

    a. Initializes the system environment by creating system environment variables.

b. Starts the Win32 subsystem (Csrss.exe). Here, Windows switches the display output from text mode to graphics mode.

c. Starts the Windows Logon Manager (Winlogon.exe), which in turn starts the Services Control Manager (Services.exe) and the Local Security Authority (Lsass.exe) and waits for a user to log on.

d. Creates any additional paging files that are required.

e. As necessary, performs delayed renaming of in-use files that were updated in the previous session.

6. The Windows Logon Manager waits for a user to log on. The logon user interface and the default credential provider collect the user name and password and pass this information to the Local Security Authority for authentication.

7. The Windows Logon Manager runs Userinit.exe and the Windows Explorer shell. Userinit.exe initializes the user environment by creating user environment variables, running startup programs, and performing other essential tasks.

Knowing this event sequence can help you identify the source of startup problems. Keep the following in mind:

- If your computer fails during the Power On Self Test's preliminary configuration, the likely cause of the problem is hardware failure or a missing device.

- If your computer fails during the setup initialization, the likely cause of the problem is the firmware configuration, the disk subsystem, or the file system.

- If your computer fails during the boot loader process, BCD data, improper OS selection for loading, or an invalid boot loader are the likely cause of the problem.

- If your computer fails during kernel and HAL initialization, driver or service configuration or service dependencies are the likely cause of the problem.

- If your computer fails before logon and during Session Manager setup, the graphics display mode, system environment, or component configuration are the likely cause of the problem.

Understanding how your computer resumes is equally important. During a resume from sleep, standby, or hibernation, your computer's advanced power settings determine how the computer turns itself back on. A computer's motherboard chipset, firmware, and operating system must support Advanced Configuration and Power Interface (ACPI) for the related advanced power state features to work. ACPI-aware components track the power state of the computer. An ACPI-aware operating system can generate a request that the system be switched to a different power state, and the firmware interface responds by enabling the requested power state.

The six different power states range from S0 (completely powered on and fully operational) to S5 (completely powered off). Everything in between is a sleep state. S1, S2, and S3 are low-power consumption states in which some or all contexts are maintained in memory. S4 is the no-power hibernate state in which context data is written to disk.

Motherboard chipsets support specific power states. One motherboard might support the S0, S1, S4, and S5 states, whereas another might support the S0, S1, S3, S4, and S5 states. As a computer user, you don't need to know the exact specifics of each state. Just remember this:

- S0 means the computer is on.
- S1, S2, and S3 mean the computer is in a sleep state but still using some power.
- S4 means the computer is hibernating and not using power.
- S5 means the computer is off.

Your computer's firmware interface has related power management settings. You can use After Power Failure, AC Recovery, or a similar setting to specify what the computer does after a power failure. If you want the computer to remain off after power is restored, set the computer to stay off. If you want the computer to go back to the state it was in before power failed, set the computer to use the last state. If you want the computer to turn itself on after a power failure, set the computer to power on.

Another power option you may see is Wake On LAN From S5 or Auto Power On. This type of option determines the action taken when the system power is off and a power management wake event occurs. If you configure this option, you'll be able to specify whether the computer stays off or powers on.

You may also have control over whether S1 or S3 suspend mode is used. From a user perspective, it really doesn't matter whether S1 or S3 is used. However, from a computer perspective it matters a lot, and you'll only want to switch modes if you are trying to correct a resume problem. For example, if your computer is having problems resuming from a sleep state, a troubleshooting option may involve changing the suspend mode.

If you encounter startup problems just prior to or after logon, the issue is probably related to a misconfigured service or startup application. To temporarily resolve this so you can log on, you can disable services and startup applications, as discussed later in this chapter.

Customizing Startup and Boot Configuration

Windows 7 provides the Startup And Recovery dialog box, the System Configuration utility, and the BCD Editor to help you modify the boot configuration and the startup process. The Startup And Recovery dialog box and the System Configuration utility are the easiest to use. Although a command-line professional may want to tune a computer with the BCD Editor, you can use the other tools to perform essentially the same tasks without all the fuss.

During startup of the operating system, you can press F8 or F12 to access the Advanced Boot Options menu and then use this menu to select one of several advanced startup modes. Although these advanced modes don't make permanent changes to your computer, you can use them to enable boot and logon when it otherwise isn't possible; then when you are logged on, you can make any necessary changes to repair your computer.

Fine-Tuning Startup and Recovery Settings

One of the easiest ways to control the way your computer starts is to configure startup options by using the Startup And Recovery dialog box. The related options set the default operating system, how long to display the list of available operating systems, and how long to display recovery options when needed. You can optimize these settings to speed up the startup process by reducing wait times while also ensuring that you can access advanced options, which may be necessary for troubleshooting and recovery.

You access and configure startup options by completing the following steps:

1. Click Start, type **SystemPropertiesAdvanced** in the Search box on the Start menu, and then press Enter to open the System Properties dialog box with the Advanced tab selected.

2. Under Startup And Recovery, click Settings to display the Startup And Recovery dialog box, shown in Figure 3-1.

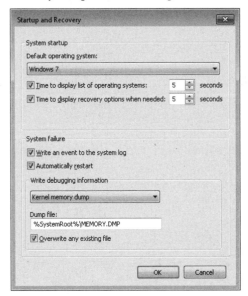

FIGURE 3-1 Configuring startup and recovery options

3. If your computer has multiple operating systems, use the Default Operating System list to specify the operating system that you want to start by default.

4. Specify the display interval for the operating system list by selecting the Time To Display List Of Operating Systems check box and setting the desired interval in seconds. To speed up the startup process, you might use a value of 5 seconds.

5. Specify the display interval for the recovery options list by selecting the Time To Display Recovery Options When Needed check box and setting the desired interval in seconds. Again, to speed up the startup process, you might use a value of 5 seconds.

6. Under System Failure, select Write An Event To The System Log if you want to record events related to system failure. If you want your computer to automatically restart after a failure, select Automatically Restart.

7. Save your settings by clicking OK twice.

Changing Your Computer's Boot Configuration

As you've seen, the Startup And Recovery dialog box makes it easy to set basic startup options. To configure more advanced options and fine-tune the startup process, you can use the System Configuration utility (Msconfig.exe). Although you typically use this utility during troubleshooting, you also can use the utility to dig down deep into startup processes and change the way startup works.

The System Configuration utility is available on the Administrative Tools menu, and you can also access it by clicking Start, typing **msconfig.exe** in the Search box, and then pressing Enter. As shown in Figure 3-2, this utility has the following tabs:

- **General** Allows you to configure normal startup, diagnostic startup, or selective startup
- **Boot** Allows you to control the way to enable various Safe Boot modes and the way that individual startup-related processes work
- **Services** Allows you to enable or disable system services
- **Startup** Allows you to enable or disable startup processes
- **Tools** Allows you to access various system management tools

You should know several important things about using the System Configuration utility:

- If you make changes on the Boot, Services, or Startup tabs, the Selective Startup option and related suboptions are automatically selected on the General tab.
- You should usually remove your selective or diagnostic options when you are finished troubleshooting your computer's problem. After you restart the computer and resolve any problems, access the System Configuration utility again, restore the original settings, and then click OK.
- You must specifically elect to make changes permanent. Otherwise, your changes will be lost when you go back to normal startup.

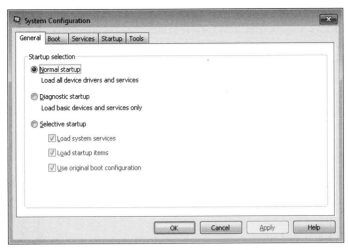

FIGURE 3-2 Fine-tuning startup with the System Configuration utility

Using the Selective and Diagnostic Startup Modes

Normal is the default startup mode. Normal startup ensures that Windows 7 loads all system configuration files and device drivers and runs all startup applications and enabled services. If your computer isn't performing properly or is generating errors at startup, you can use diagnostic or selective startup to try to determine the cause of the problem.

You use diagnostic startup to troubleshoot system problems. In diagnostic mode, your computer loads only basic device drivers and essential services. When you start the system in diagnostic mode, you can modify system settings to resolve configuration problems.

You use selective startup to identify problem areas in your computer's configuration. Selective startup is a modified boot configuration. Here, your computer only uses the system services and startup items you specify, which can help you identify settings that are causing system problems and correct them as necessary.

You can enable and use selective or diagnostic startup by completing these steps:

1. Click Start, type **msconfig**, and then press Enter to display the System Configuration utility, shown in Figure 3-2.

2. On the General tab, select either Diagnostic Startup or Selective Startup. If you choose Selective Startup, specify the items that you want your computer to use. Your choices are:

   - **Load System Services** Sets the computer to load Windows services on startup. If you select this option, use the settings on the Services tab to specify which services are started.

- **Load Startup Items** Sets the computer to run applications designated for startup at boot time. If you select this option, you can enable and disable startup applications by using the options on the Startup tab.
- **Use Original Boot Configuration** Sets the computer to process the original boot configuration on startup instead of one you've created by modifying the boot settings with the System Configuration utility.

3. When you are ready to continue, click OK, and then reboot your computer. If you have problems rebooting your computer, restart the system in Safe Mode and repeat this procedure. Safe Mode appears automatically as an option after a failed boot.

Changing the Way Your Computer Boots

Windows 7 uses the Windows Boot Manager and a boot application to start the operating system. For troubleshooting, you can use the options on the System Configuration utility's Boot tab to control the boot partition, boot method, and boot options used by the operating system.

When your computer has multiple operating systems, you can specify that an operating system other than the current one should be used simply by clicking the related operating system entry. When working with operating system entries, you can select the following options:

- **Set As Default** Sets the currently selected boot partition as the default partition. The default partition is selected automatically if you don't choose another option before the timeout interval.
- **Timeout** Sets the amount of time the computer waits before using the default boot partition.
- **Delete** Deletes an operating system entry. As the entry cannot be easily re-created, only delete an entry if absolutely necessary.

The Boot tab has other options as well, including:

- **Advanced Options** Allows you to set boot options for number of processors, maximum memory, PCI locking, and debugging.
- **Safe Boot** Sets the computer to start in Safe Mode, with additional flags for minimal, network, and alternate shell minimal boots. After you successfully boot your computer in Safe Mode, you can modify settings to resolve any configuration problems.
- **No GUI Boot** Sets the computer to boot to the Windows prompt, which doesn't load the graphical components of the operating system. Booting to the prompt is useful when you are having problems with the video and graphical components of Windows 7.
- **Boot Log** Turns on boot logging so that key startup events are written to an event log.

- **Base Video**   Forces the computer to use video graphics adapter (VGA) display settings. Use this mode when you are trying to resolve display settings, such as when the display mode is set to a size that the monitor cannot display.

- **OS Boot Information**   Starts the computer using verbose output so that you can view the details of startup activities prior to the loading of Windows graphical components.

All changes you make are stored as modified boot configuration data by the System Configuration utility. After you make changes and click OK, you can restart the computer to apply the changes temporarily. To go back to a normal startup after you've made and applied changes, you must start the utility, select Normal Startup on the General tab, and then click OK. You must then restart the computer so that the normal settings are used.

To make the standard or advanced boot options you've selected permanent, you must select the Make All Boot Settings Permanent check box on the Boot tab before clicking OK. In most cases, you won't want troubleshooting or debugging options to be permanent, so be sure to clear these options first.

Disabling Startup Applications and Services for Troubleshooting

Slow startup and errors experienced during startup can sometimes be related to applications and services run at startup. When you believe that an application loaded at startup is causing problems with your computer, you can disable the program from starting and reboot your computer. If the problem is no longer present, you might have identified the problem and can remedy it by permanently disabling the automatic startup of the program. If the problem still occurs, you can try disabling other startup applications to see if this resolves the problem.

You can disable startup applications by following these steps:

1. Open the System Configuration utility. On the Startup tab, all applications that run automatically at startup are listed by name, command path, and registry location.

2. Clear the check box next to any application that you do not want to load at startup. Make sure you only disable programs that you've identified as potential problems, and do so only if you know how they are used by the operating system.

3. Click OK. You must restart your computer to check the changes, so if you are prompted to restart the system, click Yes. Otherwise, restart manually. Repeat this procedure as necessary to identify the program causing the system problems. If you can't identify an application as the cause of the problem, a Windows component, service, or device driver might be causing the problem you are experiencing.

If disabling a startup application resolves the problem, you can then permanently disable the startup application or check with the application vendor to see if an updated executable is available.

You can troubleshoot problems with system services in a similar way:

1. Open the System Configuration utility. The Services tab displays a list of all services installed on the computer, the origin of each service, and the state of each service, such as Running or Stopped.

2. Clear the check box next to any service that you do not want to run at startup. Make sure you only disable those services that you've identified as potential problems, and do so only if you know how they are used by the operating system.

3. Click OK. You must restart the computer to check the changes, so if you are prompted to restart the system, click Yes. Otherwise, restart the computer manually. Repeat this procedure as necessary to identify the service causing the problem. If you can't identify a service as the cause of the problem, a Windows component, startup application, or device driver might be causing the problem you are experiencing.

If disabling a service resolves the problem, you can then permanently disable the service or check with the service vendor to see if an updated executable is available for the service.

Performing an Advanced or Safe Mode Boot

Windows 7 needs access to specific system files to start properly. If the required files are missing or corrupt, your computer won't start and you'll need to use the Startup Repair tool to try to resolve your computer's problem. Most of the time, repairing a damaged or missing file will fix such an issue; sometimes, you might need to continue troubleshooting to diagnose and resolve a deeper issue.

Usually a computer fails to start because something has changed and your computer doesn't like the change. For example, you might have installed an update for a device driver that caused a system-wide conflict or failed partway through. Or a program you installed might have modified the system's configuration in such a way that prevents normal startup. Whatever the cause of the problem, you can try to resolve it using safe mode.

In safe mode, Windows 7 loads only basic files, services, and drivers, including those for the mouse, monitor, keyboard, mass storage, and base video. The monitor driver sets the basic settings and modes for the computer's monitor, and the base video driver sets the basic options for the computer's graphics card.

Because safe mode loads a limited set of configuration information, it can help you troubleshoot problems. When you have finished using safe mode, be sure to restart the computer using a normal startup. You will then be able to use the computer as you normally would.

Several Safe Mode options are available. The option you use depends on the type of problem you're experiencing. The main options are:

- **Repair Your Computer** Runs the Startup Repair tool, which you can use to repair damaged or missing system files that are preventing startup, as well as to perform other recovery tasks.

- **Safe Mode** Starts the computer with only basic files, services, and drivers during the initialization sequence. The drivers loaded include those for the mouse, monitor, keyboard, mass storage, and base video. No networking services or drivers are started.

- **Safe Mode With Networking** Starts the computer with basic files, services, and drivers, as well as services and drivers needed to start networking.

- **Safe Mode With Command Prompt** Starts the computer with basic files, services, and drivers, and then starts a command prompt instead of the Windows 7 graphical interface. No networking services or drivers are started. Start the Explorer shell from the command-line interface by pressing Ctrl+Shift+Esc to open Task Manager, clicking File, clicking New Task (Run) to open the Create New Task dialog box, typing **explorer.exe,** and then clicking OK.

- **Enable Boot Logging** Turns on boot logging to create a record of all startup events in the log files.

- **Enable Low Resolution Video** Turns on low-resolution (640 × 480) display mode, which is useful if the system display is set to a mode that can't be used with the current monitor.

- **Last Known Good Configuration** Starts the computer in Safe Mode using registry information that Windows 7 saved at the last working shutdown. Only the HKEY_CURRENT_CONFIG (HKCC) hive is loaded. This registry hive stores information about the hardware configuration with which you previously and successfully started the computer.

- **Disable Automatic Restart On System Failure** Prevents Windows from restarting after a crash. If you don't set this option, Windows will restart automatically after a crash.

- **Disable Driver Signature Enforcement** Starts the computer in Safe Mode without enforcing digital signature policy settings for device drivers. This can temporarily resolve a startup problem related to a device driver with an invalid or missing digital signature. After your computer is started, you can resolve the problem permanently by getting a new driver or changing the driver signature enforcement settings.

You can start a computer in Safe Mode by completing the following steps:

1. If the computer is running but has started with errors, click Start. On the Start menu, click the Shut Down options button, and then click Restart.

2. During startup, press F8 to access the Advanced Boot Options menu.

NOTE If the computer has multiple operating systems or you've installed the Recovery Console, you'll see the Windows Boot Manager screen. Select Windows 7 as the operating system, and then press F8.

3. Use the arrow keys to select the mode you want to use, and then press Enter.

4. If a problem doesn't reappear when you start in Safe Mode, you can eliminate the default settings and basic device drivers as possible causes. Begin your troubleshooting by looking at newly added devices or updated drivers. Use Safe Mode to remove the devices, reverse the updates, or install different versions of driver software. Restart your computer to test your changes.

5. If you are still having a problem starting the system normally and suspect that problems with hardware, software, or settings are to blame, go back to Safe Mode and try using System Restore to undo previous changes.

Customizing Boot Configuration with the BCD Editor

The BCD store contains information required by your computer to locate and load the operating system. There is a single entry for the Windows Boot Manager and one Windows Boot Loader entry for each instance of Windows 7, Windows Vista, or a later version of Windows installed on the computer. On a computer with other operating systems, such as Windows XP, you'll also see a legacy operating system entry.

Windows Boot Manager is itself a boot loader application. There are other boot loader applications as well, including:

- **Bootsector**   The Windows Boot Sector Application
- **Fwbootmgr**   The Firmware Boot Manager
- **Ntldr**   The boot loader for legacy operating systems
- **Osloader**   The boot loader for Windows Vista or later operating systems
- **Resume**   The Windows Resume Loader

You access and manage the BCD store by using the BCD Editor (Bcdedit.exe). The BCD Editor is a command-line utility that requires elevated administrator privileges to perform management tasks. You can use the BCD Editor to view the entries in the BCD store by following these steps:

1. Click Start, point to All Programs, and then click Accessories.

2. Right-click Command Prompt, and then click Run As Administrator.

3. To view the entries in the BCD store, type **bcdedit** at the command prompt.

4. To view the available commands, type **bcdedit /?** at the command prompt.

REAL WORLD   The BCD Editor is an advanced command-line tool for IT professionals. If you make a mistake with the BCD Editor, your computer could end up in a nonbootable state, and you would need to initiate recovery. Because of this, only make changes when you are absolutely certain they will work.

Whenever you work with the BCD Editor, you work with the system BCD store, which contains the operating system boot entries and related boot settings. References in the BCD store can be specified by globally unique identifiers (GUIDs), such as {1cafd2de-e035-11dd-bbf6-bdebeb67615f}, as well as by well-known identifiers, such as {bootloadersettings}.

Table 3-1 shows well-known identifiers and their usage. Both well-known identifiers and GUIDs are enclosed in curly braces. GUIDs have dashes as well.

TABLE 3-1 Well-Known Identifiers

IDENTIFIER	USAGE
{badmemory}	Contains the global RAM defect list that can be inherited by any boot application entry.
{bootloadersettings}	Contains the collection of global settings that should be inherited by all Windows Boot Loader application entries.
{bootmgr}	Indicates the Windows Boot Manager entry.
{current}	Represents a virtual identifier that corresponds to the operating system boot entry for the operating system that is currently running.
{dbgsettings}	Contains the global debugger settings that can be inherited by any boot application entry.
{default}	Represents a virtual identifier that corresponds to the boot manager default application entry.
{emssettings}	Contains the global Emergency Management Services settings that can be inherited by any boot application entry.
{fwbootmgr}	Indicates the firmware boot manager entry. This entry is used on EFI systems.
{globalsettings}	Contains the collection of global settings that should be inherited by all boot application entries.
{hypervisorsettings}	Contains the hypervisor settings that can be inherited by any operating system loader entry.
{legacy}	Indicates the Windows Legacy OS Loader (Ntldr) that can be used to start Windows operating systems earlier than Windows Vista.
{memdiag}	Indicates the memory diagnostic application entry.

IDENTIFIER	USAGE
{ntldr}	Indicates the Windows Legacy OS Loader (Ntldr) that can be used to start operating systems earlier than Windows Vista.
{ramdiskoptions}	Contains the additional options required by the boot manager for RAM disk devices.
{resumeloadersettings}	Contains the collection of global settings that should be inherited by all Windows resume-from-hibernation application entries.

The BCD Editor provides separate commands for creating, copying, and deleting entries in the BCD store. You can use the /create command to create identifier, application, and inherit entries in the BCD store. The syntax is:

```
bcdedit /create Identifier /d "Description"
```

where Identifier is a well-known identifier for the entry you want to create, such as:

```
bcdedit /create {ntldr} /d "Pre-Windows Vista OS Loader"
```

You can create entries for specific boot loader applications as well, including:

- **Bootsector** Sets the boot sector for a real-mode application
- **OSLoader** Loads Windows Vista or later
- **Resume** Resumes the operating system from hibernation
- **Startup** Identifies a real-mode application

The syntax for creating entries for boot load applications is:

```
bcdedit /create /application AppType /d "Description"
```

where AppType is one of the previously listed application types, such as:

```
bcdedit /create /application osloader /d "Windows Vista"
```

You delete entries in the system store by using the /delete command and the following syntax:

```
bcdedit /delete Identifier
```

If you are trying to delete a well-known identifier, you must use the /f command to force deletion, such as:

```
bcdedit /delete {ntldr} /f
```

The /cleanup option is implied by default whenever you delete BCD entries. This option cleans up any other references to the entry being deleted to ensure that the data store doesn't have invalid references to the removed identifier. Entries are removed from the display order as well, and this could result in a different default operating system being set. To delete the entry and clean up all other references except the display order entry, you can use the /nocleanup command.

Other BCD Editor commands you can use include:

- **/set** Used to set additional options and values for entries
- **/deletevalue** Used to delete additional options and values for entries
- **/displayorder** Used to change the display order of boot managers associated with a particular Windows Vista or later installation
- **/default** Used to change the default operating system entry
- **/timeout** Used to change the timeout value associated with the default operating system
- **/bootsequence** Used to boot to a particular operating system one time and then revert to the default boot order afterward

To learn more about subcommands and how they are used, type **bcedit**, type the subcommand name, and then type **/?**. For example, to learn how to use the /set subcommand, type **bcdedit /set /?**.

Resolving Restart or Shutdown Issues

Normally, you shut down or restart Windows 7 by clicking Start, clicking the Options button to the right of the power and lock buttons, and then clicking Restart or Shut Down as appropriate. Sometimes, however, Windows 7 won't resume, shut down, or restart normally, and you must try to resolve the problem.

Recovering from a Failed Resume

Windows 7 creates a snapshot of the current state of the computer whenever your computer enters sleep mode or hibernates. Windows Resume Loader handles sleep and hibernate operations. With sleep mode, this snapshot is created in memory and then read from memory by the resume loader when you wake the computer. With hibernate mode, this snapshot is written to disk and then read from disk by the resume loader when you wake the computer.

Your computer may have a problem resuming for any of a variety of reasons that may include errors in the snapshot, physical errors in memory, and physical disk errors. Whatever the problem, Windows Resume Loader prompts you with a warning message similar to the following:

```
Windows Resume Loader
The last attempt to restart the system from its previous location
failed. Attempt to restart again?

Continue with system restart
Delete restoration data and proceed to system boot.

Enter=choose
```

The resume prompt gives you two options. You can try to continue with system restart, or you can delete restoration data and proceed to system boot. If you select Continue With System Restart, Windows Resume Loader attempts to reload the system state again. If you select Delete Restoration Data And Proceed To System Boot, Windows Resume Loader deletes the saved state of the computer and restarts the computer. Although a full restart will typically resolve any problem, you'll lose any work that wasn't saved before the computer entered sleep or hibernate mode.

Forcing Your Computer to Shut Down

When there are unsaved files, locked processes, or both, your computer will not log off and shut down immediately. Instead, you'll see a related prompt listing the files and processes that are causing the problem. With unsaved files, you'll usually want to save the open files and then exit the related program so that you can resume logging off and shutting down. With locked processes, you can wait for Windows to resolve the problem, either by getting a response from the program that allows Windows to close the program or by waiting until the timeout period has elapsed and stopping the program, which allows you to log off and shut down the computer.

That's the way your computer *should* work, but sometimes things go wrong. If you can't log off and shut down the normal way, you may need to press Ctrl+Alt+Delete to display the Windows screen and then click Start Task Manager. In Task Manager, click the Applications tab and look for an application that is not responding. If you find one, click it, and then click End Task. If the application fails to respond to the request, you'll see a prompt that allows you to end the application immediately or cancel the end task request. Click End Now.

If this doesn't solve the problem, you can try shutting down or restarting the computer. Press Ctrl+Alt+Delete and click the Shutdown button, or click the Shutdown Options button, and then click Restart. If this still doesn't work, you can perform a hard shutdown by pressing and holding the computer's power button or by unplugging the computer. If you force the computer to shut down, the Windows Error Recovery screen should be displayed automatically the next time you start the computer. You then have the option of starting the computer in one of several Safe Modes or using normal startup. After you start your computer, you may want to run Check Disk, as discussed in Chapter 8, "Optimizing Performance Tips & Techniques," to check for errors and problems that might have been caused by the hard shutdown.

Repairing a Computer to Enable Startup

Windows 7 includes the Startup Repair tool to automatically detect corrupted system files during startup and guide you through automated or manual recovery. The Startup Repair tool attempts to determine the cause of the startup failure by using startup logs and error reports, and then attempts to fix the problem automatically. If the Startup Repair tool is unable to resolve the problem, it restores your computer to the last known working state and provides diagnostics information and support options for further troubleshooting.

Every Windows 7 computer has a Window Recovery Environment (Windows RE) partition by default. This partition is created automatically when the operating system is installed. As a result, if your computer fails to shut down properly, the Windows Error Recovery screen is shown automatically the next time you start the computer. You then have the option of starting the computer in one of several Safe Modes or using normal startup. If your computer fails to start properly, the Windows Error Recovery screen is shown automatically the next time you try to start the computer. You then have the option of running the Startup Repair tool or using normal startup.

The Startup Repair tool checks for problems preventing your computer from starting. If problems are found, the tool tries to repair them to enable startup. The automated troubleshooting and repair process can take several minutes. During the first phase of the repair, you can click Cancel to exit.

If Startup Repair doesn't find common problems, you have the option of performing a system restore or canceling the restore. Clicking Restore starts System Restore. Clicking Cancel returns to the startup repair process, and the Startup Repair tool attempts to make repairs using advanced techniques.

If Startup Repair is successful, your computer will start. If Startup Repair is unable to find and correct problems, you'll see a note about this and will be able to send more information about the problem to Microsoft to help find solutions in the future. After selecting the option to send or not send information, you return to the Startup Repair dialog box.

To access advanced repair options, click the related link and follow the prompts to continue troubleshooting. Otherwise, click Finish. You may want to disconnect any external devices that you've recently connected to your computer and then try to start your computer again. Otherwise, ask your network administrator or your computer manufacturer for help.

Corrupted system files aren't the only types of problems that can prevent proper startup of the operating system. Many other types of problems can occur, but most of these problems occur because something on the system has changed. Often you can resolve startup issues using Safe Mode to recover or troubleshoot system problems. When you are finished using Safe Mode, be sure to restart the computer using a normal startup. You will then be able to use the computer as you normally would. See "Performing an Advanced or Safe Mode Boot," earlier in this chapter, for more information.

CHAPTER 4

Organizing, Searching, and Indexing

One of your computer's most important functions is to make it possible for you to create and store everything—from documents and pictures to songs, videos, and program data files. Windows 7 gives you many options for helping you organize, search for, and index these files. To get the most out of the available features, you need to master Windows Explorer and Windows Search.

Exploring Your Computer in New Ways

Out of all the components of the Windows operating system that you'll use, you'll spend more time using Windows Explorer. Every time you browse files and folders on your computer, you use Windows Explorer—whether you specifically open an Explorer window or you use the Open command in an application, such as Microsoft Word. Control Panel, the Computer window, the Network window, and even the Recycle Bin are different views for Windows Explorer.

As Figure 4-1 shows, Windows Explorer has an Address bar for quickly navigating disks and folders, a Search box for fast searches, and the following view panes:

- **Navigation** Helps you quickly access favorites, libraries, homegroups, your computer, and your network. Drag any folder to Favorites to quickly create a shortcut to it; right-click and select Remove to delete a favorite. Libraries are predefined and provide a combined view of folders related to specific types of media.

- **Contents** Provides the main working pane and shows the contents of your selected drive or folder. Use the View button and View options to control whether item details, lists, or icons are shown.

- **Details** Shows information about a selected item. The details provided depend on the item selected and are different for drives, folders, documents, songs, videos, and shortcuts. Hide or show the Details pane by clicking Organize, clicking Layout, and then clicking Preview Pane.

- **Preview** Shows a preview of your selected document, picture, song, video, or other file type, as long as a preview control is available and configured for that file type. Use the Show/Hide Preview button to display or hide the Preview pane.

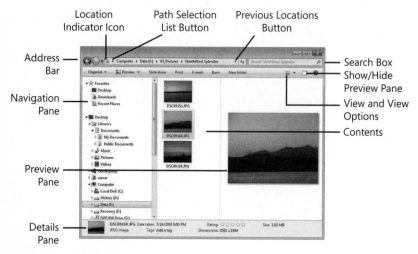

FIGURE 4-1 Exploring the drives, folders, and files on your computer

Address Bar Tips and Techniques

Every view of Windows Explorer, whether Control Panel, the Computer window, the Network window, or the basic Explorer view, has an Address bar that displays your current location as a series of links separated by clickable options buttons.

The address path includes a Location Indicator icon, a Path Selection list button, Location Path entries, and a Previous Locations button. Location Path entries allow you to determine the current location. In the example shown in Figure 4-1, the location is:

Computer → Data (E:) → 03_Pictures → NorthWest Splendor

This tells you that the absolute path followed to get to the current location is E:\03_Pictures\Northwest Splendor on your computer (as opposed to a network location). When you are working with network paths in the Network window, you have quick access to network locations and shared resources on remote servers. Click the Network entry in the path to display a list of remote computers and network resources. Click the name of a remote computer or network resource to list its shared resources.

You won't always see a full path, however. Many times, you'll see a relative or abbreviated path, such as when you follow a shortcut or browse to a path that cannot be fully listed. A relative or abbreviated path is indicated by the left-pointing chevron (<<), as shown in this example:

« 02_History → Availability → New Materials

This tells you that the relative or abbreviated path of the current location is 02_History\Availability\New Materials.

For ease of reference, I refer to Explorer's relative and absolute paths as navigation paths. When a navigation path is being displayed, you can always display the actual system path by clicking the Location Indictor icon or an empty area of the address path. For example, if I click the relative path listed previously, my computer shows the system path as E:\02_History\Availability\New Materials.

By default, the system path is selected, so you can copy it simply by pressing Ctrl+C. To display the navigation path again (instead of the system path), press Esc. Double-click the icon to view the same drop-down list provided by the Previous Locations button.

To the right of the Location Indicator icon is the Path Selection list button, which provides access to the available base locations. Selecting a base location allows you to quickly access key Windows Explorer views and perform related tasks. You can access:

- **Your Account**   Accesses your personal folder. Additional options on the taskbar may include: Open, for opening a selected folder or file; Share With, for sharing a selected folder or file; Burn, for burning a selected folder or file to CD or DVD; and Include In Library, for adding a selected folder or file to your library.

- **Control Panel**   Accesses Control Panel tools and task links. You can then work with Control Panel options by using Category, Large Icons, or Small Icons view.

- **Desktop**   Accesses the desktop as a folder and allows you to view and work with all the shortcuts, files, and folders stored on the desktop. Use this view to help you clean up the clutter on your desktop or to find items on a cluttered desktop.

- **Libraries**   Accesses the base page for libraries on your computer. Additional options on the taskbar may include: Open, for opening the selected folder or file; Share With, for configuring sharing options for your computer; Burn, for burning a selected folder or file to CD or DVD; and New Library, for creating a custom library.

- **Computer**   Accesses your computer's hard disk drives and devices with removable storage. Taskbar options may include: System Properties, for accessing the System console in Control Panel; Uninstall Or Change A Program, for opening the Installed Programs console in Control Panel;

Map Network Drive, for mapping a shared folder on a computer; and Properties, for accessing a selected item's Properties dialog box.

- **Network**   Accesses the base page for the computers and devices on your network. Additional options on the taskbar may include: Search Active Directory, for when you are at the office and want to find available resources; Network And Sharing Center, for configuring network sharing and printing options; Add A Printer, for adding a printer; and Add A Wireless Device.

- **Recycle Bin**   Displays files marked for deletion in the Recycle Bin. Additional options on the taskbar may include: Empty The Recycle Bin, for permanently deleting all Recycle Bin items; Restore All Items, for restoring all Recycle Bin items to their original locations; and Restore This Item, for restoring a selected item to its original location.

The final control on the Address bar is the Previous Locations button, which provides a list of locations you've accessed recently. This location list can include folder locations, network drive locations, and web addresses. You can jump to a recently accessed location quickly by clicking the Previous Locations button and then clicking the desired location.

Keyboard Tips and Techniques for Windows Explorer

Putting Windows Explorer to work for you requires much more than simply learning to navigate the Address bar like a pro. Next, you need to learn about keyboard shortcuts that can make your everyday computing tasks easier. I'll go through the shortcuts you're likely to find the most helpful. The secret to your success is in being even more selective. Identify the techniques that will help you the most and commit those techniques to memory.

NOTE   Generally, the keyboard shortcuts in this section work only when the main pane is the selected focus for Windows Explorer. This means you must be working in the main pane for the shortcut to work.

Most people who've worked with Windows for a while know that you right-click an item and select Properties to display the item's properties. There are two other ways to do the same thing:

- Hold the Alt key and then double-click the item.
- Select the item and then press Alt+Enter.

In Chapter 1, I discussed customizing the Start menu and pinning programs. Although you normally want only programs on the Start menu, you can pin documents, songs, videos, and most other types of files to the Start menu as well. You do this by holding Shift, right-clicking the file, and then clicking Pin To Start Menu, a menu option that is hidden when the Shift key is not pressed. Another hidden option displayed when you hold Shift before right-clicking a file is Copy As Path, which is used to copy the full path of the file to the clipboard.

With folders, holding Shift before right-clicking reveals three hidden options:

- **Copy As Path**   Copies the full path of the folder to the clipboard.
- **Open Command Windows Here**   Opens a command prompt with the initial path set to the folder location.
- **Open In New Process**   Opens the folder in a separate process. Otherwise, by default, all Explorer windows run in the same process.

Windows Explorer has several other shortcuts for working smarter with folders as well. When a folder is selected in the window:

- Press Alt and the Up Arrow key to jump to the parent folder of that folder.
- Press Enter to view the folder's contents. Then you can press Alt and the Left Arrow key to go back.
- Press Ctrl+Shift+E to expand the folder tree so that the selected folder is at the bottom of the Navigation pane.

Windows Explorer has Forward and Back buttons as well as a Recent Pages drop-down list. These buttons are easy enough to use, but you also can press Backspace to go back through the Recent Pages list. Within a folder, you can press a letter key or string of characters to quickly jump to the first file or folder starting with that letter or character string. For example, if you press C, Windows Explorer jumps to the first file or folder that starts with C. If you type **Chr**, Windows Explorer jumps to the first file or folder that starts with Chr.

> **NOTE**   Folder And Search Options can modify the way quick select works. Instead of jumping to the file or folder that starts with the letters you type, you also can configure Windows Explorer to enter the text in the Search box and begin a search of the current folder.

The Preview pane is handy, but it can take up a lot of workspace. You can quickly display or hide the Preview pane by pressing Alt+P. My preference is to not use the Preview pane at all. Instead of turning previews on and off, I hold Ctrl and use the mouse scroll button to cycle through the view settings. That way, I can quickly go from a detailed listing to a small, medium, or large icon listing.

Windows Explorer provides a variety of ways to work with files and folders. You can press Ctrl+Shift+N to create a new folder. You can press F2 to rename a currently selected file or folder. You can press Shift+Del to permanently remove a selected file or folder (bypassing the Recycle Bin).

Hold Ctrl and click to select multiple files and folders or deselect files and folders previously selected one by one. If you want to select a range of files or folders instead, click the first item to select it, hold Shift, and then click the final item. Now all items in the range, from the first item to final item, will be selected.

Other ways to select multiple files include:

- Using selection rectangles to select a group of files. Simply click an empty area near the first file and drag to draw a selection box around all the files you want to select.

- Using Ctrl and the spacebar to select individual items. While holding Ctrl, use the Up and Down Arrow keys to move through a list of items and press the spacebar to select or deselect an item.

- Using Shift and the spacebar to select a range of items. Here, find the first item using the Up and Down Arrow keys. Next, hold Shift and use the arrow keys to expand your selection.

Customizing Windows Explorer

Windows Explorer settings control many aspects of the Windows operating system. Everything from whether hidden files are displayed to whether a single click opens an item and many dozens of other core options are configured by modifying settings in Windows Explorer.

Fine-Tuning Folder Views

Windows Explorer identifies folders as having mostly documents, mostly music, mostly pictures, or mostly videos and then uses a template to set their default view when opened. Although there is a general template for folders containing mixed media, the default view for most folders is based on the Documents template.

The Documents template is a basic template that doesn't have any media extensions. In contrast, the Music, Pictures, and Videos templates have media extensions that allow you to preview the media and work with the media in different ways. With music, the Music template is used and the Music pane provides the Play, Play All, and Burn options.

For folders that contain mostly pictures, the Pictures template is used. Each picture is displayed with a thumbnail that you can use for quick browsing, and a Picture pane provides Preview, Slide Show, Print, and Burn options. For folders that contain mostly videos, the Videos template is used. When you are working with videos, the Video pane provides Play, Play All, and Burn options.

If you have write permissions on a folder, you can customize the folder's default view. You also can apply a favorite view to all folders of that type on the system. The folder view settings that you use are seen by all users who access the system, either locally or remotely.

You can configure custom views for folders by following these steps:

1. In Windows Explorer, right-click the folder you want to customize, and then select Properties.

2. Click the Customize tab, as shown in Figure 4-2.

3. In the Optimize This Folder For list, choose the template you want to use, such as Pictures. To apply the view to subfolders of this folder, choose Also Apply This Template To All Subfolders.

4. Customize the folder preview, and then click OK to save your settings. By default, a folder shows a folder icon with thumbnails for the first few files as a folder preview. If you want, you can set a specific background picture or other file that will be used instead of the thumbnails. Click Choose File, and then use the Browse dialog box to select the picture or other file you want to use as part of the folder's preview.

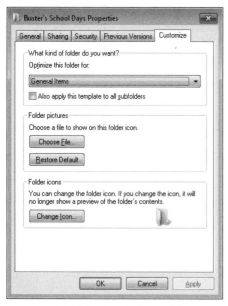

FIGURE 4-2 Optimizing default views for folders using templates

Instead of setting folder views one by one, you can apply a custom view to all the folders of a particular type or restore the default view to these folders. To apply a custom view to all the folders of a particular type, complete the following steps:

1. In Windows Explorer, select the folder you want to work with. Use the options in the View list or on the View menu to configure the folder view that you want to use, such as Large Icons.

2. Click Organize, and then click Folder And Search Options.

3. In the Folder Options dialog box, select the View tab.

4. Do one of the following, and then click OK:

   ■ To apply the current folder view to all folders of this type, click Apply To Folders.

   ■ To restore all folders of this type to their default view, click Reset Folders.

You also may want all folders regardless of type to use the same default view. You can do this by following these steps:

1. In Windows Explorer, right-click the folder you want to work with, and then select Properties.

2. Select the Customize tab. Under Optimize This Folder For, choose General Items. Click OK.

3. In Windows Explorer, select the folder. Use the options in the View list or on the View menu to configure the folder view that you want to use, such as Large Icons.

4. Click Organize, and then click Folder And Search Options.

5. On the View tab, click Apply To Folders to apply the current folder view to all folders of this type. When prompted to confirm, click Yes.

6. Repeat this procedure four times, once each for the Documents, Pictures, Music, and Videos templates. In step 2, choose Documents, Pictures, Music, or Videos as appropriate.

Customizing Folder Options

You control the way Windows Explorer works by using settings in the Folder Options dialog box. Access this dialog box in Windows Explorer by clicking Organize, and then clicking Folder And Search Options. General tab and View tab options are shown in Figure 4-3. Use Table 4-1 to help you understand how each option works, and then choose the configuration option that is best for the way you want Windows Explorer to work.

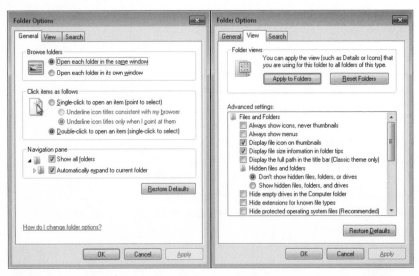

FIGURE 4-3 Optimizing Windows Explorer settings for the way you work

TABLE 4-1 Folder Options for Windows Explorer

TAB/ SETTING	WHEN SELECTED, WINDOWS EXPLORER ...	WHEN NOT SELECTED, WINDOWS EXPLORER ...
GENERAL		
Open Each Folder In The Same Window	Opens subfolders that you access in the same window.	Opens subfolders that you access in a new window.
Single-Click To Open An Item	Selects an item when you point to it and opens the item when you click once.	Selects an item when you click it; opens the item when you double-click it.
VIEW		
Always Show Icons, Never Thumbnails	Shows large thumbnail images of the actual content for pictures and other types of files. When folders have many pictures, this option can slow down the display because Windows Explorer has to create the thumbnail representation of each image.	Does not create thumbnails. Instead, Windows Explorer shows the standard file and folder icons.
Always Show Menus	Always shows the menu bar, providing quick access to the menus. (You can also toggle this option by clicking Organize, pointing to Layout, and then selecting Menu Bar.)	Hides the menu bar; you must elect to display it by pressing the Alt key.
Display File Icon On Thumbnails	Adds file icons to thumbnails it displays.	Displays thumbnails without file icons.
Display File Size Information In Folder Tips	Displays a tooltip showing the creation date and time, the size of the folder, and a partial list of files when you move the mouse pointer over a folder name or folder icon.	Displays a tooltip showing the creation date and time when you move the mouse pointer over a folder name or folder icon.

TAB/ SETTING	WHEN SELECTED, WINDOWS EXPLORER ...	WHEN NOT SELECTED, WINDOWS EXPLORER ...
Display The Full Path In The Title Bar	When you press Alt+Tab to access the flip view, displays the actual file path instead of the folder name when you move the mouse pointer over a Windows Explorer window.	When you press Alt+Tab to access the flip view, displays the folder name when you move the mouse pointer over a Windows Explorer window.
Hidden Files And Folders	Displays hidden files, folders, or drives.	Does not display hidden files, folders, or drives.
Hide Empty Drives In The Computer Folder	Displays information about empty drives in the Computer window.	Does not display information about empty drives in the Computer window.
Hide Extensions For Known File Types	Does not display file extensions for known file types.	Displays file extensions for known file types.
Hide Protected Operating System Files	Does not display operating system files.	Displays operating system files. Hidden operating system files are also referred to as super hidden files.
Launch Folder Windows In A Separate Process	Runs in a separate process each time it is opened. Although this requires more memory and generally slows down the process of opening new windows, it also means that each instance is independent of the others. Thus, if one instance crashes or hangs, it generally will not affect other instances of Windows Explorer.	Windows runs all instances of Windows Explorer in the same process. Although this saves memory and generally speeds up the process of opening new windows, it also means that all instances of Windows Explorer are dependent on each other. As a result, if one instance crashes, they all crash, and if one instance is in a pending or wait state, all instances could become locked.
Show Drive Letters	Displays drive letters as part of the information on the Locations bar.	Does not display drive letters as part of the information on the Locations bar.

TAB/ SETTING	WHEN SELECTED, WINDOWS EXPLORER ...	WHEN NOT SELECTED, WINDOWS EXPLORER ...
Show Encrypted Or Compressed NTFS Files In Color	Lists encrypted files and compressed files using different colors. Normally, encrypted files are displayed with green text and compressed files are displayed with blue text.	Does not distinguish among encrypted, compressed, and normal files.
Show Pop-Up Description For Folder And Desktop Items	Shows tooltips with additional information about a file or folder when you move the mouse over the file or folder.	Does not show tooltips with additional information about a file or folder when you move the mouse over the file or folder.
Show Preview Handlers In Preview Pane	When the Preview pane is visible, displays previews of selected files and folders.	When the Preview pane is visible, does not display previews of selected files and folders.
Use Check Boxes To Select Items	Displays check boxes that you can use to select files.	Allows you to select files, folders, and other items using only the standard selection techniques such as click, Shift+Click, and Ctrl+Click.
Use Sharing Wizard	Uses the File Sharing wizard for configuring file sharing.	Uses the advanced file sharing options. When you try to share files, you'll need to click Advanced Sharing on the Sharing tab so that you can configure permissions, caching, and connections settings separately.
When Typing Into A List View, Automatically Type Into The Search Box	When you are working with the list view and press a letter key, enters the text you type into the Search box.	When you are working with the list view and press a letter key, selects the first file or folder with that letter.

Searching and Indexing Your Computer

Your computer's drives probably have hundreds or even many thousands of documents, pictures, music, videos, and more, stored until you one day want to access them. The more digital stuff you have, the harder it is to find what you're looking for right now. This is where the Windows 7 search and indexing features come in.

Windows Search Essentials

Whether you perform a search using the Search box on the Start menu or the Search box in Windows Explorer, the Windows Search service performs the search. The way Windows Search service looks for the file you are trying to find depends on where you are searching. All views of Windows Explorer have a Search box, allowing you to search Control Panel, Network, Computer, Desktop, Public, and Recycle Bin locations. The Start menu also has a Search box.

By default, you must click in the Search box prior to typing your search text. This means a basic search requires two steps:

1. In an Explorer window or related view, access the start location for your search.

2. Click in the Search box, and then enter the search text.

> **NOTE** The When Typing Into A List View option determines whether you have to click in the Search box before entering search text. By default, you must click in the Search box, but if you enable Automatically Type Into The Search Box, any text you type into a list view is entered automatically in the Search box.

A general search involves Windows Search service matching the search text to words that appear in the title of any file or file folder, the properties of any indexed file or folder, and the contents of indexed documents in the currently selected folder and its subfolders. For example, if you were to search the C:\Documents folder, the Windows Search service would search C:\Documents and all its subfolders. It would not search other folders or other locations.

Results are returned to the Results Pane in Windows Explorer, and the Address bar is updated to reflect that you are viewing search results. The search results themselves are displayed in Content view by default. In this view, search results normally are listed by name, date modified, size, authors, and tags. If you click the Location Indicator icon on the left side of the address path, you'll see the actual search text passed to the Windows Search service.

After the Windows Search service completes a search in the selected location, it automatically begins another search if you enter additional search text or if you change the search text. You can stop a search in progress at any time by clicking the Stop button—the red X on the right side of the Address bar. You can repeat a search by clicking the Refresh button.

Understanding Localized Searches

By default, only a few specific locations on a computer are indexed, including personal profile folders and the Start menu. The automatic indexing of selected files and folders is a key feature of Windows 7 that improves the search results and helps speed up the search process.

A localized search involves Windows Search service checking a specific location. When you perform a search in Control Panel, the search is localized to the names of related utilities and tasks. When you perform a search in the Network window, the search is localized to the names and ownership information for computers and devices listed therein.

Similarly, searches of Desktop and Recycle Bin are localized. For the desktop, Windows Search service matches against file names, file type information, and folder details related to items stored therein. For the Recycle Bin, Windows Search service matches against item names and original folder locations.

A Start menu search is much more broad than you might think. Windows Search service looks at the names of programs, the names of utilities, and tasks in Control Panel, and then looks at information related to indexed files in other locations.

Whenever you search in the Computer window, a drive folder, or any subfolder of a drive, you are performing a localized search as well. If the location you are searching is indexed, Windows Search service checks its index to try to find what you are looking for, and the search process is usually fairly quick. If the location you are searching isn't indexed, Windows Search service will try to find what you are looking for without the benefit of an index, and the search process can be fairly slow.

By default, with a non-indexed location, Windows Search service tries to match your search text against file and folder names of the currently selected folder and any subfolders of that folder. As shown in Figure 4-4, you'll know you are searching a non-indexed location because of a warning message that states:

Searches might be slow in non-indexed locations.... Click to add to index.

NOTE By right-clicking the message panel and selecting Add To Index, you can mark the location for indexing. This will speed up future searches but won't help with the current search.

As shown in the figure, the Search Again In panel provides options for quickly repeating the search, including:

- **Libraries**   Matches your search text against file and folder names in all library locations.
- **Custom**   Allows you to choose a search location from the default locations list, which includes Desktop, Libraries, Home Group, Computer, Network, Control Panel, and your personal folders.
- **File Contents**   Searches the current location again while looking at the contents of files in that location.

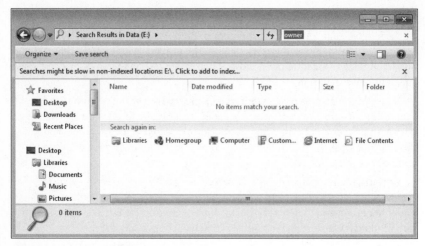

FIGURE 4-4 Searching non-indexed locations

Fine-Tuning Windows Search

You can improve your search results by using the advanced search options and features built into Windows 7. These additional advanced features include search options for fine-tuning the search results and advanced filters that allow you to search in new ways, as well as options for managing which files and folders are indexed and saved searches that allow you to easily repeat custom searches.

Customizing Search Options

Search options control the way the Windows Search service searches your computer. The search service has several default behaviors. In indexed locations, the Windows Search service searches file names and contents. This means that it will look for matches to your search text in file names and folder names, file properties and folder properties, and the textual contents of files.

In nonindexed locations, the Windows Search service searches file names only. This means it will look for matches to your search text only in file names and folder names. It will not look for matches to your search text in file and folder properties, or in the textual contents of files.

Additionally, the service doesn't use natural language searches or search compressed files, but it does search subfolders of a selected location and allows partial matches. Disallowing natural language searches means you can't enter natural language questions as part of your search. Excluding compressed files means that .zip, .cab, and other archival files aren't searched. Partial matching means that the service matches your search text to part of a word or phrase rather than to whole words only.

Although these default behaviors work well for most people, they are limiting. You can customize the search options by completing the following steps:

1. In Windows Explorer, click Organize on the menu bar and then click Folder And Search Options. Select the Search tab in the Folder Options dialog box, as shown in Figure 4-5.

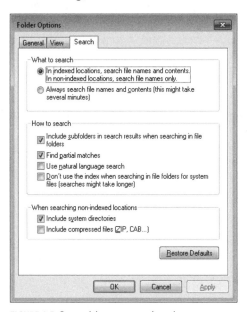

FIGURE 4-5 Customizing your search options

2. Under What To Search, select the option that best describes how you want the search to work. To have the Windows Search service search contents only for indexed locations, select the first option. To have the Windows Search service always search file names and contents even in non-indexed locations, select the second option.

   REAL WORLD   If you always want the service to search contents, you force the Windows Search service to ignore whether a folder is indexed when searching. This does not mean that indexes won't be used, however. When indexes are available, the Windows Search service will use them. When indexes aren't available, the Windows Search service will not be able to use indexes to speed up the search process, and this can result in slow searches.

3. Under How To Search, use the following options to configure how searches work:

   ■ **Include Subfolders In Search Results When Searching In File Folders**   When selected, the Windows Search service searches the selected location and all its subfolders. This lets you search entire drives or complete folder structures. When not selected, the Windows Search service searches only the selected location and does not search subfolders.

- **Find Partial Matches**   When selected, the Windows Search service returns results for partial matches as well as whole-word matches. When not selected, the Windows Search service performs whole-word searches only.

- **Use Natural Language Search**   When selected, the Windows Search service allows you to enter search text as a question you might ask someone. For example, you could enter the question, "Where is the Pictures folder?" and the Windows Search service would know that you are looking for a folder named Pictures or folders containing pictures. When not selected, the Windows Search service uses all the text you enter for matching, as discussed previously.

- **Don't Use The Index When Searching In File Folders For System Files**   When selected, the Windows Search service ignores indexes when searching in file folders for system files. This forces the Windows Search service to examine the current state of system files, but it can be extremely slow. When not selected, the Windows Search service uses indexes to speed up the search process if indexes are available.

NOTE   Normally, system files are not indexed because they aren't searched very often. However, if you are an advanced user or administrator and have indexed system files, you'll want to use the index when searching (in most cases).

4. Under When Searching Non-indexed Locations, specify whether the Windows Search service includes system locations, compressed files, or both when searching nonindexed locations. If you often zip files and folders or create file cabinets (cab files) and then delete the originals, you are likely to improve your search results by including compressed files in searches.

5. Click OK to save your search options.

Performing Advanced Searches with Filters

You won't always know the name of a resource you are looking for. Instead, you may know only the approximate size of the file, the general type of file, or when you last modified the file. In these cases, you can narrow your results using search filters, such as:

- **Datemodified:**   Filters the search results according to the date on which files and folders were last modified. You can specify a range of dates. For example, you could enter Datemodified:09/02/2011..12/31/2011 to specify the date as being between 09/02/2011 and 12/31/2011. A set of predefined flags also can be used to set a general time period, such as Datemodified:Yesterday or Datemodified:Earlier This Week.

- **Kind:** Filters the search results according to the general kind of file, such as all picture or video files. A set of predefined flags can be used to set the general kind, but unlike other flags these must be separated from the filter identifier with an equal sign, such as Kind:=Calendar or Kind:=Video.

- **Type:** Filters the search results according to the file type label or file extension. For example, you could use type:"MP3 Format Sound" or type:mp3 to search for .mp3 audio files.

- **Size:** Filters the search results according to the approximate size of a file. Size flags have specific parameters, including Empty for files having zero bytes and Medium for 100 KB to 1 MB. For example, you could specify that you are searching for a file between 100 KB and 1 MB by using the filter Size:Medium.

The available search filters are based on the names of indexable properties associated with files and folders. The basic syntax for a search filter is PropertyName: where PropertyName is the property name entered without spaces followed by a colon, such as Datecreated:. You use Datecreated: in the same way as DateModified:. For example, you could use Datecreated:Yesterday as your search filter.

REAL WORLD Search filters are available in Windows Explorer, on the Start menu, and in other search boxes in Windows 7. To use these filters with other Search boxes, simply enter the filters, flags, and search parameters you want to use. For example, if you click Start and then type **kind:=video** in the Search box, you'll see a list of all the videos on your computer. If you have a lot of videos, you'll need to click See All Results to get an expanded view of the search results.

Because document files, picture files, video files, music files, and other types of files all have slightly different lists of indexable properties, they also have slightly different lists of search filters. A quick way to discover these is to follow these steps:

1. Open Windows Explorer. In the Navigation pane, click Music under Libraries.

2. In the main pane, you'll see songs listed by name, contributing artists, albums, track number, title, and type by default. Display a list of related headings by right-clicking an open area of the column headings.

3. Any of the headings shown can be used in your searches for music files. The related search filter is the heading name without spaces followed by a colon. You can learn about flags and options available with a filter by simply entering the filter in the Search box. For example, to search on bit rate, you could use the Bitrate: filter. If you enter **bitrate:** in the Search box, you'll see flags for voice and AM broadcasts, FM broadcasts, high-quality audio, and near-CD-quality audio.

4. To discover properties specific to documents, pictures, and videos, repeat this process, selecting Documents, Pictures, and Videos as appropriate instead of Music.

NOTE Although you can use any filter in any type of folder, the default folder view controls the column headings displayed by default as well as the headings that are listed when you right-click the column heading. As discussed earlier in the section "Fine-Tuning Folder Views," Windows Explorer identifies folders as having mostly documents, mostly music, mostly pictures, or mostly videos, and then uses a template to set their default view.

You can use search filters with or without keywords. If you want to perform a filtered search with a keyword, click in the search window, type the keyword or phrase, and then enter the filter. If you want to begin a search without a keyword, click in the search window and then enter the filter. Just as you can use multiple keywords, you can use multiple filters in a single search. For example, you could search using the date modified, size, and kind filters. Searches that combine multiple filters and are difficult to re-create are the ones you'll likely want to save for later reuse.

Windows Search service allows you to perform logical AND searches as well as logical OR and logical NOT searches. AND (entered in all caps) acts as an operator to match exactly two or more keywords separated by AND operators. OR (entered in all caps) acts as an operator to match any of the keywords separated by OR operators. NOT (entered in all caps) acts as a selective operator to match one keyword but not another.

You use AND to perform complex searches that match multiple parameters. If file content searching is enabled, you could search for files containing the keyword Chicago and the keyword Miami using:

```
chicago AND miami
```

Here, only files containing both keywords are returned. Because the logical AND operation is implied whenever you enter multiple keywords in the Search box, you also could have simply entered:

```
chicago miami
```

You could limit the search to matching file names by using the Name: filter, such as:

```
name:better AND name:food
```

Here, only files whose name includes both *better* and *food* are returned. Logical OR operations can be handy as well. For example, you could search for either *better* or *food* or both *better* and *food* using:

```
Name:better OR Name:food
```

Here, files whose name includes either *better* or *food* are returned. To look for files who name includes *better* but not *food*, you could use the search parameters:

```
Name:better NOT Name:food
```

Searching by Kind or Type of File

When you are working with libraries and certain other folders, the Kind: and Type: filters are implied when you click in the Search box. These filters are also available when you are working with other folders, but you must enter the filter to use them. In either case, any file with a kind or type that matches your parameters is returned in the search results.

The kinds of files you can search for include:

- **Calendar**   Filters the search results so that only calendar items are included.
- **Communication**   Filters the search results so that only calendar, email, contact, and instant message items are included.
- **Contact**   Filters the search results so that only contact items are included.
- **Document**   Filters the search results so that only document files are included.
- **E-mail**   Filters the search results so that only email messages are included.
- **Feed**   Filters the search results so that only messages from RSS feeds are included.
- **Folder**   Filters the search results so that only folders are included.
- **Game**   Filters the search results so that only game data and other game files are included.
- **Instant Message**   Filters the search results so that only instant messages are included.
- **Journal**   Filters the search results so that only journal entries are included.
- **Link**   Filters the search results so that only links are included.
- **Movie**   Filters the search results so that only movie files are included.
- **Music**   Filters the search results so that only music files are included.
- **Note**   Filters the search results so that only note files are included.
- **Picture**   Filters the search results so that only pictures are included.
- **Program**   Filters the search results so that program files are included.
- **Recorded TV**   Filters the search results so that recorded television programs are included.
- **Saved Search**   Filters the search results so that saved searches are included.
- **Task**   Filters the search results so that tasks are included.
- **Video**   Filters the search results so that video files are included.
- **Web History**   Filters the search results so that items from your web history are included.

When performing kind or type searches, remember to enter your search keyword or keywords first and then enter the Kind: or Type: filter. For example, if you know the file you are looking for is a video and the file name includes the keyword "vacation," you could search for it by following these steps:

1. In Windows Explorer, access the top-level folder from which you want to start searching.

2. Click in the Search box. Type **vacation kind:video**, and then press Enter.

The Type: filter allows you to search for a specific type of file by its file type label or file extension. For example, if you know the file you are looking for is a .wmv file and the file name includes the keyword "home," you could search for it by following these steps:

1. In Windows Explorer, access the top-level folder from which you want to start searching.

2. Click in the Search box. Type **home type:wmv**, and then press Enter.

The Type: filter also accepts three special flags:

- **"Directory"**   Filters the search results for directories only.
- **"File Folder"**   Filters the search results for directories only.
- **"Compressed (zipped) Folder"**   Filters the search results for compressed (zipped) folders only.

If you don't use one of these special flags, any search you perform with a filter matches only files.

Searching Using Date-Related Filters

Windows Search service tracks a variety of date-related properties, including:

- **Date Accessed**   Tracks the date a file was last accessed.
- **Date Archived**   Tracks the date a file was last archived.
- **Date Last Saved**   Tracks the date a file was last saved.
- **Date Created**   Tracks the date a file was created.
- **Date Modified**   Tracks the date a file was last modified.
- **Date Sent**   Tracks the date a message was sent.
- **Date Taken**   Tracks the date a picture was taken.

Generally, they all work in the same way. When you are working with a date filter, you can select a specific date, a general date, or a range of dates to search. Any file with a date that matches your parameters is returned in the search results.

You select specific dates by using the calendar provided, as shown in Figure 4-6. The calendar displays the current day and date by default.

Select a date or date range:

◀		December, 2012			▶	
Su	Mo	Tu	We	Th	Fr	Sa
		1	2	3	4	5
6	7	8	9	10	11	12
13	14	15	16	17	18	19
20	21	22	23	24	25	26
27	28	29	30	31		

A long time ago

Earlier this year

Earlier this month

Last week

Earlier this week

Yesterday

FIGURE 4-6 Searching using date-related filters

The calendar has the several views:

- **Month** The month view is the default. While working with the month view, you can view other months in the calendar by using the right and left arrow buttons. Click and drag in the calendar to select a series of dates, such as the 5th through the 25th days of the month.

- **Year** The year view lists the months in a year. You can access the year view from the month view by clicking the month and year entry at the top of the calendar. While working with the year view, you can view other years in the calendar by using the right and left arrow buttons. Click and drag in the calendar to select a series of months, such as February through April.

- **Decade** The decade view lists the years in a 10-year period. You can access the decade view from the month view by clicking twice at the top of the calendar. While working with the decade view, you can view other decades in the calendar by using the right and left arrow buttons. Click and drag in the calendar to select a series of years, such as 2008 to 2010.

- **Century** The century view lists the 10-year periods in a particular century. You can access the century view from the month view by clicking three times at the top of the calendar. While working with the century view, you can view other centuries in the calendar by using the right and left arrow buttons. Click and drag in the calendar to select a series of decades, such as 2000–2009 or 2010–2019.

The date-related filters accept abbreviated entries as well. Using an abbreviated entry, you can directly enter the date to search. The basic syntax varies by locality. For U.S. English, the syntax is:

Mm/Dd/Yyyy

or:

Mm/Dd/Yyyy .. Mm/Dd/Yyyy

where *Mm* is a one- or two-digit value for the month, *Dd* is a one- or two-digit value for the day of the month, and *Yyyy* is a four-digit value for the year. Knowing this, you could search for pictures taken between 1/1/2011 and 12/31/2011 by following these steps:

1. In Windows Explorer, access the top-level folder from which you want to start searching.
2. Click in the Search box. Optionally, type a keyword or phrase to search on.
3. Type **Datetaken: 1/1/2011 .. 12/31/2011**, and then press Enter to begin your search.

With date-related filters, you also can use the following predefined flags:

- **Yesterday**   Searches for files and folders created yesterday.
- **Earlier this week**   Searches for files and folders created earlier in the current week.
- **Last week**   Searches for files and folders created in the previous week.
- **Earlier this month**   Searches for files and folders created earlier in the current month.
- **Earlier this year**   Searches for files and folders created earlier in the current year.
- **A long time ago**   Searches for files and folders created prior to the current year.

You can search using the predefined flags by following these steps:

1. In Windows Explorer, access the top-level folder from which you want to start searching.
2. Click in the Search box. Optionally, type a keyword or phrase to search on.
3. Type the date-related filter you want to use, such as **Datetaken:**.
4. Type the preset label or click the preset button in the Search pane, and then press Enter to begin your search.

Windows Search service also allows you to use operators. Use the equal (=) operator to get an exact date match. For example, if you know a file was created on 12/15/2011, you can use the filter:

DateCreated:=12/15/2011

You also can use the less than, greater than, less than or equal to, greater than or equal to, or not equal to operators: <, >, <=, >=, <>. For example, you could look for files modified after 01/01/2011 by entering:

```
DateModified:>01/01/2011
```

As an alternative to the Mm/Dd/Yyyy .. Mm/Dd/Yyyy syntax, you could combine > and < searches using the AND operator. For example, you could look for files modified after 01/01/2011 but before 05/31/2011 by entering:

```
DateModified:>01/01/2011 AND DateModified:<05/31/2011
```

Because the AND is always implied, you also could enter:

```
DateModified:>01/01/2011 DateModified:<05/31/2011
```

Or you could enter:

```
DateModified:(>01/01/2011 <05/31/2011)
```

This final syntax is closer to the one Windows Search service actually uses internally.

Searching Using Size-Related Filters

Windows Search service tracks a variety of size-related properties, including:

- **Dimensions:** Tracks the width and height of pictures.
- **Framewidth:** Tracks the width of frames in a video.
- **Frameheight:** Tracks the height of frames in a video.
- **Length:** Tracks the running time of songs and videos.
- **Size:** Tracks the size of the file as stored on the hard disk.

With the Dimensions: filter, you can search on the width and height of pictures. You can search using exact dimensions by using an equal sign and the dimensions in quotes, such as Dimensions:"1920 x 1020" or Dimensions:"2048 x 1536". The quotes and spaces are required to get a match. Implied in these examples is the equal (=) operator, so you also could enter Dimensions:="1920 x 1020" or Dimensions:="2048 x 1536". You also can use the less than, greater than, less than or equal to, greater than or equal to, or not equal to operators: <, >, <=, >=, <>.

The Framewidth: and Frameheight: filters can help search videos. For example, you could search for videos that are 320 x 240 by entering the search parameters:

```
framewidth:320 frameheight:240
```

Again, the equal (=) operator is implied, so you also could enter Framewidth:=320 Frameheight:=240. To search for videos with higher quality and larger frame sizes, you could use the search parameters:

```
framewidth:>320 frameheight:>240
```

Another handy size-related filter is Length:, which has the following flags:

- **Very Short** For songs and videos less than a minute.
- **Short** For songs and videos from 1 to 5 minutes in length.
- **Medium** For songs and videos from 5 to 30 minutes in length.
- **Long** For songs and videos from 30 to 60 minutes in length.
- **Very Long** For songs and videos longer than 60 minutes.

Although you could enter numeric values for length, the search won't work as you expect. This is because the length is expressed internally in fractional seconds; you can see this by clicking the Location Indicator icon in the address path.

With the Size: filter, you can specify an approximate file size. Any file with a file size approximately matching your parameters is returned in the search results. The size options are:

- **Empty** Allows you to search for empty files.
- **Tiny** Allows you to search for files of 0 to 10 KB.
- **Small** Allows you to search for files of 10 to 100 KB.
- **Medium** Allows you to search for files of 100 KB to 1 MB.
- **Large** Allows you to search for files of 1 MB to 16 MB.
- **Huge** Allows you to search for files of 16 MB to 128 MB.
- **Gigantic** Allows you to search for files over 128 MB.

The size flags allow you to quickly find files that meet specific size criteria. For example, if you know the file you are looking for is medium in size and has the keyword "staff" or "monthly," you could search for it by following these steps:

1. In Windows Explorer, access the top-level folder from which you want to start searching.
2. Click in the Search box. Type **staff OR monthly size:medium**, and then press Enter.

The Size: filter accepts abbreviated entries as well. Using an abbreviated entry, you can directly enter the size parameters for the search. The basic syntax is:

```
size: SmallestSize .. LargestSize
```

where *SmallestSize* is the smallest file size that meets your parameters and *LargestSize* is the largest file size that meets your parameters. Use kb to specify a size in kilobytes, mb to specify a size in megabytes, and gb to specify a size in gigabytes. The kb, mb, and gb labels are required. If you don't use the appropriate label, Windows Search service won't return the expected results. Here's an example of how you could search for files between 50 KB and 2 MB:

1. In Windows Explorer, access the top-level folder from which you want to start searching.
2. Click in the Search box. Type **50kb .. 2mb**, and then press Enter.

You also can use the operators discussed previously, including <, >, <=, >=, and <>. For example, to search for files smaller than 900 KB in size, you would type

Size:<900kb and press Enter to begin your search. To search for files greater than 900 KM in size, you would type **Size:>900kb** and press Enter to begin your search.

Saving Your Searches

You can save any search you perform in Windows Explorer. When you save a search, your search criteria are saved as a search folder so that you can rapidly perform an identical search in the future.

You can create a search folder by completing the following steps:

1. Perform a search, and then click Save Search on the menu bar.

2. In the Save As dialog box, accept the default name and location for the search folder or select a new save location and name.

3. Click Save to create the search folder. Searches are saved with the .search-ms file extension.

By default, saved searches are stored in the Searches folder within your personal folders. You can access a saved search at any time by clicking Start, clicking your user name on the Start menu, and then clicking Searches.

Search folders are represented by a blue icon with a magnifying glass and are listed according to the search filters you used in the Searches folder under the Saved Search heading.

When you open or double-click a search folder, the Windows Search service either retrieves the cached results of your previous search or performs a new search using the search criteria. The result is a list of matching files and folders that appear to be in the selected folder. The folder does not actually contain any files or folders, however. A search folder's only content is the associated search string.

You can work with search folders in the same way you work with regular folders. You can:

- Use Ctrl+X to cut and Ctrl+V to paste a search folder in a new location.
- Use Ctrl+C to copy and Ctrl+V to paste to create copies of search folders.
- Press Delete to remove search folders.

Although you cannot edit search folders to update the search criteria, you can delete a search folder, configure the desired search criteria, and then save the new search using the old search folder name.

Indexing Your Computer

You tell the Windows Search service about locations that should be indexed by designating them as searched locations. After you've designated a folder as an indexed location, the Windows Search service is notified that it needs to update the related index whenever you modify the contents of the folder. You can manage the indexing of your computer's files and folders by adding or removing indexed locations, specifying file types to exclude, and rebuilding indexes as necessary.

Customizing Indexed Locations

The Windows Search service indexes only a few locations by default. These locations are:

- **Internet Explorer feeds and history**   RSS feed messages and browser history are indexed for fast searching. (Specific to Internet Explorer)
- **Libraries**   Files and folders stored in any library are indexed for fast searching.
- **Microsoft Office Outlook**   Mail saved on your computer is indexed for fast searching. (Specific to Outlook)
- **Offline files**   All offline file folders are indexed for fast searching.
- **Start menu**   All menu options are indexed for fast searching.
- **Users**   All personal folders of all users of the computer are indexed for fast searching.

TIP   The quickest way to ensure that a folder is indexed is to add the folder to a library. Although application data folders are stored within user profiles, these folders are excluded from indexing by default. Because you don't want to index folders or files associated with application data, this is the desired setting in most instances.

You can add or remove indexed locations by completing the following steps:

1. Click Start, type **Indexing Options**, and then press Enter. The Indexing Options dialog box provides an overview of indexing on your computer, which includes the total number of items indexed and the current indexing state. The currently indexed locations are listed under Included Locations.

2. Select a location and then click Modify. In the Indexed Locations dialog box, click Show All Locations to display hidden locations as well as standard locations.

3. Use the options provided to select locations to index, or clear check boxes for locations you no longer want to index. Click OK to save your changes.

The locations you can index include offline file folders, Outlook, Internet Explorer history, hard disk drives, and devices with removable storage. If a node can be expanded, you'll see an open triangle to the left of the location name. Click this to expand the location. For example, you could expand Local Disk (C:) to select a folder on the C: drive.

NOTE   Some system folders are excluded from indexing and are displayed dimmed to prevent them from being selected. If you enable indexing of the entire system drive, these system folders are excluded automatically.

Including or Excluding Files by Type

Windows Search service can be configured to index file and folder names, file and folder properties, and file and folder contents. Windows Search service determines which types of files and folders to index according to the file extension.

The Windows Search service uses the information that it knows about file types and file extensions to help it index files more efficiently. Each file extension has a file filter associated with it, and this filter determines exactly whether and how files with a particular extension are indexed. For files included in the index, there are two general settings:

- **Index Properties Only**   Ensures that only the properties of the file are indexed.
- **Index Properties And File Contents**   Ensures that the properties of the file are indexed and that the contents of the file can be indexed as well, if content indexing is enabled.

You can specify file types that the Windows Search service should include or exclude when indexing files by completing the following steps:

1. Click Start, type **Indexing Options**, and then press Enter.
2. Click Advanced. On the Index Settings tab, select the Index Encrypted Files check box if you want the Windows Search service to index files that have been encrypted.
3. If you want to improve indexing of non-English characters, select the Treat Similar Words With Diacritics As Different Words check box. A diacritic is a mark above or below a letter that indicates a change in the way it is pronounced or stressed.

    NOTE   Selecting or clearing the options in Step 2 or 3 will cause the Windows Search service to completely rebuild the indexes on your computer.

4. On the File Types tab, each file extension and filter association is listed. If a file extension is selected, the Windows Search service includes files of this type when indexing. If a file extension is not selected, the Windows Search service excludes files of this type when indexing. Select or clear file extensions as appropriate.

    REAL WORLD   When you install new applications, those applications may register new filters with the Windows Search service and configure related file extensions to use these filters. If a filter isn't available and you want to add support for a particular file extension, type the file extension in the text box provided and then click Add.

5. To change the way files with a particular extension are indexed, select the file extension and then click either Index Properties Only or Index Properties And File Contents. Only change the way indexing works when you are sure the indexing configuration you've chosen works. Although you can always stop indexing the contents of a particular file type, you'll rarely want to index the contents of a file type that isn't already being indexed.
6. Click OK to save your settings.

Resolving Indexing Problems

The Windows Search service must be running for you to perform searches. The service must also be running to index files. If you suspect there's a problem with searching or indexing, you should check the status of the Windows Search service. To do this, follow these steps:

1. Click Start, type **View Local Services**, and then press Enter.

2. In the Services window, ensure the status of the Windows Search service is listed as Started. If the service isn't running, right-click Windows Search and then click Start.

Other problems you may experience with searching and indexing have to do with corrupt indexes, improper index settings, and the index location running out of space. An indicator of a corrupt index is when your searches do not return the expected results or new documents are not being indexed properly. An indicator of improper index settings is when your searches fail or the Windows Search service generates bad file errors in the event logs. An indicator of the index location running out of space is when indexing of new documents fails and there are out-of-disk-space reports in the event logs for the Windows Search service.

The Windows Search service does a good job of automatically correcting some problems with indexes. For other types of problems, you'll find error reports in the form of Windows events in the system event logs. You can correct most problems with searching and indexing by completing the following steps:

1. Click Start, type **Indexing Options**, and then press Enter.

2. Click Advanced. If you suspect your computer's indexes are corrupt, click Rebuild. Windows 7 rebuilds the indexes on your computer by stopping the Windows Search service, clearing out indexes, and then starting the Windows Search service. Indexes also may be rebuilt whenever you restart your computer.

3. By default, the Windows Search service creates indexes in the *%ProgramData%*\Microsoft folder. If the related drive is low on space or if you want to try to balance the workload by using other hard disk drives, you may want to change the index location. To do this, click Select New under Index Location. In the Browse For Folder dialog box, select the disk drive and folder in which the index should be stored, and then click OK. The next time you restart your computer or the Windows Search service, indexes will be created in the new location.

4. Click OK. In the Indexing Options dialog box, you can track the status of reindexing files by watching the number of indexed items increase. The indexing status indicates whether indexing is complete or in progress.

CHAPTER 5

Optimizing Your Computer's Software

These days, most software programs have automated setup processes that make them easy to install and run. What's not always so easy is resolving issues with 32-bit or 64-bit operating systems, resuming installation if automated setup fails, and making programs work like they're supposed to when things go wrong. To resolve issues you may encounter, you need a strong understanding of how installation works and techniques for diagnosing problems.

Diving Deep into Software Installation

Software installation and related processes have changed considerably since the days of Windows XP and earlier operating systems. Understanding these processes and related concepts will help you optimize your computer for the way you use software.

Understanding and Tweaking User Account Control

Software installation, configuration, and maintenance are processes that require elevated privileges. Elevation is a feature of User Account Control (UAC). Because of UAC, Windows 7 can detect software installation and prompt for permission or consent before allowing you to install, configure, or maintain software on your computer.

Most programs created for Windows 95, Windows 98, Windows Me, Windows 2000, and Windows XP use Setup.exe programs. Programs created for Windows Vista and later versions of Windows can use Autorun.exe or other programs, such as Startcd.exe, particularly if those programs use current versions of Windows installers. For simplicity's sake, I'll refer to setup, autorun, and similar programs as Setup programs.

Like Windows Vista, Windows 7 changes the way application access tokens are used and the way software programs write to system locations. As a result, software that you use with the operating system falls into one or two categories. The software is either said to be a UAC-compliant application or a legacy application.

Any software written specifically for the revised architecture guidelines of Windows Vista and later versions of Windows is considered a compliant application and can be certified as Windows-compliant. Applications written for Windows 7 have access tokens that describe the privileges required to run and perform tasks. UAC-compliant applications are either administrator user applications or standard user applications.

Windows 7 has only standard user accounts and administrator accounts. When you create a user in Windows 7, you choose one type of account or the other. Applications that require elevated privileges to run and perform tasks are considered administrator user applications. Administrator user applications can write to system locations of the registry and file system.

Applications that do not require elevated privileges to run and perform tasks are considered standard user applications. Standard user applications should write only to nonsystem locations of the registry and file system.

Any application written for Windows XP or an earlier version of Windows is considered a legacy application. Legacy applications run as standard user applications in a special compatibility mode that provides virtualized views of file and registry locations.

When a legacy application attempts to write to a system location, Windows 7 gives the application a private copy of the related file or registry value. Any changes are then written to the private copy, and this private copy is in turn stored in the user's profile data. If the application attempts to read or write to this system location again, it is given the private copy from the user's profile.

> **REAL WORLD** In Windows 7, the Power Users group is included only for backward compatibility, and you should use it only when you need to resolve compatibility issues with legacy applications. You access the advanced group permissions needed to add a user to this group by using the hidden User Accounts control panel (click Start, type **lusrmgr.msc** in the Search box, and then press Enter). You can also use the Computer Management administrative tool and select Local Users and Groups.

You can manage the way in which various UAC aspects work for all users of your computer through local security policy. The related settings are:

- **User Account Control: Admin Approval Mode For The Built-In Administrator Account** Controls whether users and processes running as the built-in local Administrator account are subject to Admin Approval Mode. By default, this feature is enabled, which means the built-in local Administrator account is subject to Admin Approval Mode and also subject to the elevation prompt behavior stipulated for administrators in Admin Approval Mode. If you disable this setting, users and processes running as the built-in local Administrator are not subject to Admin Approval Mode and therefore not subject to the elevation prompt behavior stipulated for administrators in Admin Approval Mode.

- **User Account Control: Allow UIAccess Applications To Prompt For Elevation Without Using The Secure Desktop**   Controls whether User Interface Accessibility (UIAccess) programs can automatically disable the secure desktop for elevation prompts used by a standard user. If you enable this setting, UIAccess programs, including Windows Remote Assistance, can disable the secure desktop for elevation prompts.

- **User Account Control: Behavior Of The Elevation Prompt For Administrators In Admin Approval Mode**   Controls whether administrators subject to Admin Approval Mode see an elevation prompt when running administrator applications, and also determines how the elevation prompt works. By default, administrators are prompted for consent when running administrator applications on the secure desktop. You can configure this option so that administrators are prompted for consent without the secure desktop, prompted for credentials with or without the secure desktop (as is the case with standard users), or prompted for consent only for non-Windows binaries. You can also configure this option so that administrators are not prompted at all, in which case an administrator is elevated automatically. No setting will prevent an administrator from right-clicking an application shortcut and selecting Run As Administrator.

- **User Account Control: Behavior Of The Elevation Prompt For Standard Users**   Controls whether users logged on with a standard user account see an elevation prompt when running administrator applications. By default, users logged on with a standard user account are prompted for the credentials of an administrator on the secure desktop when running administrator applications or performing administrator tasks. You can also configure this option so that users are prompted for credentials on the standard desktop rather than the secure desktop, or you can deny elevation requests automatically. If you deny elevation requests automatically, users will not be able to elevate their privileges by supplying administrator credentials, but this doesn't prevent users from right-clicking an application shortcut and selecting Run As Administrator.

- **User Account Control: Detect Application Installations And Prompt For Elevation**   Controls whether Windows 7 automatically detects application installation and prompts for elevation or consent. (This setting is enabled by default in Windows 7.) If you disable this setting, users are not prompted, in which case the users cannot elevate permissions by supplying administrator credentials.

- **User Account Control: Only Elevate Executables That Are Signed And Validated**   Controls whether applications must be signed and validated to elevate. If enabled, only executables that pass signature checks and have certificates in the Trusted Publisher store will elevate. Use this option only when the highest security is required and you've verified that all applications in use are signed and valid.

- **User Account Control: Only Elevate UIAccess Applications That Are Installed in Secure Locations**   Controls whether UIAccess programs must reside in a secure location on the file system to elevate. If enabled, UIAccess programs must reside in a secure location under *%SystemRoot%*\Program Files, *%SystemRoot%*\Program Files(x86), or *%SystemRoot%*\Windows\System32.

- **User Account Control: Run All Administrators In Admin Approval Mode**   Controls whether users logged on with an administrator account are subject to Admin Approval Mode. By default, this feature is enabled, which means administrators are subject to Admin Approval Mode and also subject to the elevation prompt behavior stipulated for administrators in Admin Approval Mode. If you disable this setting, users logged on with an administrator account are not subject to Admin Approval and therefore are not subject to the elevation prompt behavior stipulated for administrators in Admin Approval Mode.

- **User Account Control: Switch To The Secure Desktop When Prompting For Elevation**   Controls whether the elevation prompt is displayed on a user's interactive desktop or the secure desktop. By default, this feature is enabled, which means all elevation prompts go to the secure desktop regardless of the prompt behavior settings for administrators and standard users. If you disable this setting, the prompt behavior settings for administrators and standard users determine whether the secure desktop is used for elevation requests.

- **User Account Control: Virtualize File And Registry Write Failures To Per-User Locations**   Controls whether file and registry virtualization is on or off. Because this setting is enabled by default, error notifications and error logging related to virtualized files and registry values are written to the virtualized location rather than the actual location to which the application was trying to write. If you disable this setting, the application will silently fail when trying to write to protected folders or protected areas of the registry.

You can configure security policy settings for UAC by following these steps:

1. Click Start, type **secpol.msc** in the Search box, and then press Enter.

2. In the Local Security Policy window, under Security Settings, expand Local Policies and select Security Options, as shown in Figure 5-1.

3. Double-click the setting you want to work with, make any necessary changes, and then click OK. Repeat this step to modify other security settings as necessary.

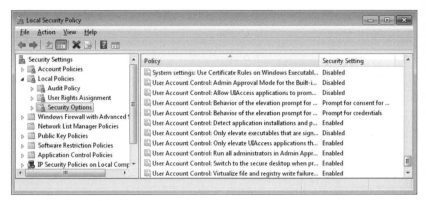

FIGURE 5-1 Accessing UAC settings

Understanding Autorun and Tweaking AutoPlay

The software installation process starts when you trigger the AutoPlay or Autorun process. AutoPlay or Autorun then starts the Setup program that manages the installation process. Part of the installation process involves validating your user credentials and the software's compatibility with Windows 7.

AutoPlay options determine how the operating system handles files of various types on various media. You can configure separate AutoPlay options for each type of BD, CD, DVD, and other media your computer can handle. With software, the AutoPlay options allow you to install or run the related program or open a folder to view related files in Windows Explorer. A program's Autorun file determines what file to run to start the installation process.

You can customize AutoPlay options by completing the following steps:

1.   Click Start, type **Autoplay** in the Search box, and then press Enter.

2.   As shown in Figure 5-2, do one of the following:

   ■   Use the lists under Media to set the default AutoPlay option for each type of media. For example, you can configure software and games to Install Or Run Programs From Your Media.

   ■   Clear the Use AutoPlay For All Media And Devices check box if you don't want to use AutoPlay. Note that this will disable AutoPlay for both media and devices.

3.   Click Save to save your settings.

NOTE   The various AutoPlay options require Windows to determine the type of disc and media you've inserted, which can sometimes slow the disc recognition process. "Ask me every time" is a safe choice, because it requires you to decide before any action is taken.

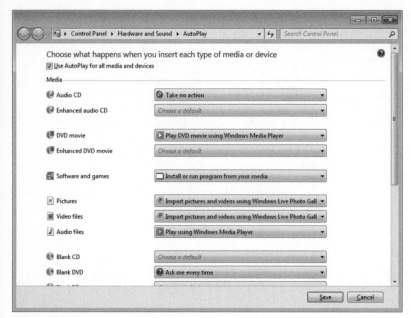

FIGURE 5-2 Configuring AutoPlay options

> **REAL WORLD** If you don't like using AutoPlay for media, you may still want to use
> AutoPlay for devices. Instead of disabling AutoPlay completely, you can set the default
> value for all media as Take No Action, which allows you to still use AutoPlay with devices.

When AutoPlay is enabled, Windows 7 checks for a file named Autorun.inf or
a similar file, such as Startcd.ini, whenever you insert a CD or DVD into a CD or DVD
drive. For software applications and games, the Autorun file identifies the Setup
program and related installation parameters that should be used to install the
software or game.

Almost all Autorun files are text-based. This means that you can view their
contents in any standard text editor, such as WordPad or Notepad. Most Autorun.inf
files are similar to the following example.

```
[autorun]
OPEN=SETUP.EXE
ICON=SETUP.EXE,1
SHELL=OPEN
DisplayName=Microsoft Office 2010
```

This Autorun.inf file tells Windows 7 to open a file named Setup.exe. Because
the file is an executable (.exe), Windows 7 knows this is a program to run.
The Autorun.inf file also specifies an icon to use, and the program's display name.

As long as AutoPlay is enabled, you can retrigger the default action by ejecting and then reinserting the installation media. With the media inserted, you can also trigger the default action for media by double-clicking the drive's icon.

Although Autorun.inf usually is configured to run a Setup program, this isn't always the case. When AutoPlay triggers this Autorun.inf file, Windows 7 opens a file named Default.htm in Internet Explorer.

```
[autorun]
OPEN=Autorun\ShelExec default.htm
```

Startcd.ini and similar files expand and improve upon the basic options provided in Autorun.inf files. As an example, Startcd.ini can be used to define a splash window containing graphics, text, and selectable menu options. Consider the following example.

```
[Option1]
Caption=&iEngine Setup
DataText1=Install Windows iEngine.
DataText2=Install the Windows iEngine. The Windows iEngine contains a set
of tools to help you manage remote computers over the Internet.
DataText3=Once the installation is complete, click Start, click All
Programs, click Windows iEngine, click Documentation and open the
Windows iEngine User's Guide.
Cmd=iEngine.exe
CmdParameters=/i "%RootDir%\ieng.msi"
ErrorSoln=Check to make sure that this file is accessible. If it is not
accessible, try opening the file from its original location.
Action=OPEN
```

This example defines the window caption, display text, command to run, run action, and error text for the first option on a splash window of a program called Windows iEngine. The Open action is what tells the operating system to try to open the related file. Again, because this file is an executable, Windows 7 knows to run the program, which starts the installation process.

How Windows Installer and Program Compatibility Work

Most software applications have a Setup program that uses Windows Installer, InstallShield, or Wise Installer. The job of the installer program is to track the installation process and make sure that the installation completes successfully.

Before installing software, you determine whether it is compatible with Windows 7. The software packaging or the developer's website should provide this information. Because only administrator users can install software, you must either install software using an account with administrator privileges or provide administrator permissions when prompted. Administrator privileges are required to change, repair, and uninstall software as well.

Windows 7 includes the Program Compatibility Assistant, which is a safeguard against software incompatibilities. Prior to performing any software installation, Windows 7 launches the Program Compatibility Assistant to check for known compatibility issues.

If an issue is found, the assistant notifies you about the problem and provides possible solutions. You can then allow the assistant to reconfigure the application for you or ignore the recommendations. Although the assistant is helpful, it can't detect or prevent all compatibility issues, and you may need to manually configure compatibility settings.

REAL WORLD   You should not use the Program Compatibility Assistant or the related wizard to install older virus detection, backup, or system programs. Why? These programs may attempt to modify your computer in a way that is incompatible with Windows 7, and this could prevent Windows 7 from starting.

Diagnosing a problem your computer is having as a compatibility issue isn't always easy. For deeper compatibility issues, you may need to contact the software developer's technical support department. The support staff may not be able to resolve some issues without time to study the problem.

Remember that if an installation fails, the installer is also responsible for restoring your computer to its original state by reversing all the changes made by the Setup program. This works great in theory, but you may encounter problems, particularly when installing legacy programs. These older programs won't have, and won't be able to use, the latest features of newer versions of installer programs, and as a result, they sometimes are unable to uninstall a program completely.

Because a partially uninstalled program can mean disaster for your computer, you should ensure that your computer is configured to use System Restore. The installers for most current programs automatically trigger a restore point creation before making any changes to your computer. However, the installers for legacy programs may not, so you may want to manually create a restore point before you install an older program on your computer. This way, if you run into problems, you'll be able to restore your computer to its original state.

How 64-Bit Software Works

We are in the midst of a changeover to 64-bit computing, so software developers are increasingly producing both 32-bit and 64-bit versions of their programs. Some software developers are even shifting entirely to 64-bit and not making 32-bit versions of their programs available.

To use 64-bit programs, your computer must run a 64-bit version of Windows. The fastest way to determine whether your computer is running a 64-bit version of Windows is to use the System Information utility. Click Start, type **System Information**, and then press Enter. Review the System Type listed with the system summary information, as shown in Figure 5-3. If the system type is listed as an x64-based PC, your computer is running a 64-bit version of Windows. If the system type is listed as an x86-based PC, your computer is running a 32-bit version of Windows.

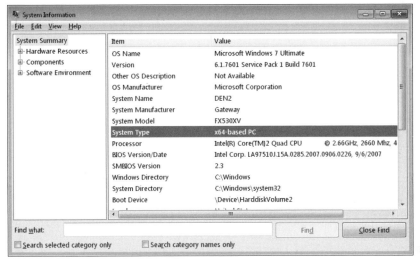

FIGURE 5-3 Determining your Windows version

Just because your computer is running a 32-bit version of Windows doesn't mean your computer can't run a 64-bit version. The System Information utility shows your processor type. Check the manufacturer's website to determine whether the processor supports 64-bit technology. If you've installed Windows PowerShell, you can determine whether a computer supports a 64-bit operating system by using the Name and Description properties of the Win32_Processor object. Here is an example:

```
get-wmiobject -class win32_processor | format-list name,
description

name        : Intel(R) Core(TM)2 Quad CPU          @ 2.66GHz
description : x64 Family 6 Model 15 Stepping 7
```

When you are working with a 64-bit operating system, you need to remember the following:

- You can't install 16-bit applications.

- By default, Windows installs 64-bit programs in subfolders of the Program Files folder.

- By default, Windows installs 32-bit programs in subfolders of the Program Files (x86) folder.

- Registry keys for 32-bit programs are found in HKEY_LOCAL_MACHINE\ SOFTWARE\Wow6432Node.

- Registry keys for 64-bit programs are found in HKEY_LOCAL_MACHINE\ SOFTWARE.

Some programs may have both a 32-bit version and a 64-bit version. Most of the time, you'll get better performance with the native 64-bit version of a program, but not always. For example, for several years Adobe chose not to release a 64-bit version of its flash player. This meant you could only view flash in 32-bit browsers.

If you encounter compatibility issues with a 64-bit program, you can try running the 32-bit x86 version of the program instead. If you are running 64-bit Windows and don't know whether a program is 32-bit or 64-bit, start the program, and press Ctrl+Alt+Delete to start Task Manager. On the Processes tab, 32-bit processes are identified with "*32" after the process name. If you don't know the name of the program's process, right-click the application on the Applications tab and select Go To Process.

Installing and Running Your Software

The operating system provides a framework for you to install, configure, and run software. However, the software itself must provide the Setup program. The Setup program and the installer work together to help you install, configure, and run your software. The Setup program also provides the components necessary for reconfiguring or removing the software.

Software can be provided as a download or on installation media. If you downloaded a program from the Internet, it is probably in a ZIP or self-extracting executable file, and you can install the program by following these steps:

1. In Windows Explorer, extract the program's setup files using one of the following techniques:

   - For a program distributed in a .zip file, right-click the file and select Extract All. This displays the Extract Compressed (Zipped) Folders dialog box. Click Browse, select a destination folder, and then click OK. Click Extract.

   - For a program distributed in a self-extracting executable file, double-click the .exe file to extract the setup files. You'll see one of several types of prompts. If you're prompted to run the file, click Run. If you're prompted to extract the program files or select a destination folder, click Browse, select a destination folder, and then click OK. Click Extract or OK as appropriate.

2. In Windows Explorer, browse the setup folders and find the Setup program. Double-click the Setup program to start the installation process.

3. When Setup starts, follow the prompts to install the software. If the installation fails and the software used an installer, follow the prompts to allow the installer to restore your computer to its original state. Otherwise, exit Setup and then try rerunning Setup to either complete the installation or uninstall the program.

If your software is distributed on installation media, you can install your software by following these steps:

1. Insert the media disc into your computer's CD or DVD drive.

2. If Windows 7 displays the AutoPlay dialog box, click Run Setup.exe or a similar option under Install or Run Program. When Setup starts, follow the prompts to install the software, and skip the remaining steps.

3. If Windows 7 doesn't display the AutoPlay dialog box, click Start, and then click Computer. In the Computer window, double-click the CD or DVD drive.

4. If Windows 7 detects the software's Setup program (using Autorun.inf or a similar file), you are then prompted for permission or consent to run the Setup program. If Windows 7 doesn't detect the software's Setup program, the contents of the disc are displayed in Windows Explorer. Double-click the Setup program.

5. When the Setup program starts, follow the prompts to install the software. If the installation fails and the software has an installer, follow the prompts to allow the installer to restore your computer to its original state. Otherwise, exit Setup and then try rerunning the Setup program to either complete the installation or uninstall the program.

With older programs, the Program Compatibility Assistant may not be able to determine whether the software installed properly. If this happens, the assistant may prompt you to specify whether the software installed correctly. If you indicate that the program didn't install properly, the assistant gives you a chance to retry the installation using compatibility mode settings that it thinks will work.

You can run installed software by selecting the software's menu option or double-clicking its desktop shortcut. If you encounter problems installing or running the software, be sure to read the "Making Software Work Like You Want It To" section of this chapter.

As you work with software, remember that Windows components aren't software that you install. They are features that can be turned on and off, and they include Indexing Service, Internet Explorer, Windows Media Player, Windows Media Center, and Windows DVD Maker.

You turn Windows features on or off by following these steps:

1. Click Start, type **optionalFeatures.exe**, and then press Enter.

2. To turn features on, select feature check boxes. To turn features off, clear feature check boxes.

3. When you click OK, Windows 7 reconfigures components as appropriate for any changes you've made. You may need to restart your computer. If prompted to do so, save your work and then click Restart.

Making Software Work Like You Want It To

Most programs written for Windows Vista or later will run well on a computer running Windows 7. It's the older programs—the ones written for earlier releases of Windows—that can make life difficult when you try to install and run them. The problems you are likely to encounter depend on when a program was written; the sections that follow examine issues related to various types of older programs, starting with 16-bit programs and programs written for MS-DOS.

Making MS-DOS and 16-Bit Software Work

Sometimes a favorite program or required utility at work won't install or run, and when you try to find out why, you discover that the program was written for MS-DOS or uses 16-bit programming. Programs written for MS-DOS and 16-bit environments present a unique problem. Why? Because 64-bit versions of Windows 7 won't install or run MS-DOS or 16-bit programs. Thirty-two-bit versions of Windows can install and run some MS-DOS and 16-bit programs, but not others.

As a result, trying to install MS-DOS and 16-bit programs on your computer can be unpredictable. You might hear that someone got a 16-bit program to run on his computer. If so, you might be thinking, why won't this 16-bit program install and run? The hidden gotcha is that 32-bit Windows versions can only run MS-DOS or 16-bit programs that don't require direct access to your computer's hardware and don't require 16-bit drivers. If the MS-DOS or 16-bit program you are trying to install relies on either or both, it won't install or run.

Whether you are using 64-bit Windows or you want to install an incompatible MS-DOS or 16-bit program on 32-bit Windows, the workaround is the same. It's called Windows XP Mode, and I discuss it in the "Using Windows XP Mode" section of this chapter.

If an MS-DOS or 16-bit program installs on your computer running 32-bit Windows 7 without Windows XP Mode, there are some things you need to know. First, whenever you run an MS-DOS or 16-bit program, Windows 7 performs some compatibility tasks automatically. In MS-DOS and 16-bit file systems, file names are restricted to eight characters with a three-character file extension, such as Program2.exe. This naming convention is often referred to as the 8.3 file-naming rule or the standard MS-DOS file-naming rule. MS-DOS and 16-bit folder paths are similarly restricted. The same is not true for Windows 7. The file systems used with Windows 7 support long file names of up to 255 characters. To ensure compatibility for MS-DOS and 16-bit programs, Windows 7 translates between long and short file names to ensure that your computer's file systems are protected when an MS-DOS or 16-bit program modifies files and folders.

Second, Windows 7 runs these MS-DOS and 16-bit programs using a virtual machine that mimics the 386-enhanced mode used by Windows 3.0 and Windows 3.1, which are the original operating systems that these programs were developed for. Windows 7 runs multiple MS-DOS and 16-bit programs within a single virtual machine. Although each program is managed using a separate thread, all the programs share a common memory space. Therefore, if one MS-DOS or 16-bit program fails, it usually means others running on the computer will fail as well.

To prevent cascading failure, you can configure each MS-DOS or 16-bit program to run in a separate memory space. Although this uses additional memory, you'll usually find that the programs are more responsive. An added benefit of using separate memory spaces is that you'll be able to run multiple instances of each program.

You can configure a 16-bit or MS-DOS program to run in a separate memory space by completing the following steps:

1. Right-click the program's shortcut or menu option, and then select Properties. This opens the program's Properties dialog box.

2. On the Shortcut tab, note the name of the program's executable file and click Open File Location. This opens the folder in which the program's executable is stored in Windows Explorer.

3. Right-click the program's executable file, and then select Properties.

4. On the Compatibility tab, configure the desired compatibility settings, and then click OK to save the changes.

Controlling Software Availability

Most software written for Windows 2000 and later installs and is made available to all users of the computer. Some software prompts you to choose whether you want to install the software for all users or only for the currently logged-on user. Other programs, including those written for Windows 98 and earlier, install themselves only for the current user and can only be used in this way.

Software that installs and is made available to all users is said to have an all-user configuration. The software installer writes to areas of the registry and file system available to all users and makes its program shortcuts available to all users.

Software that installs and is made available to the currently logged-on user is said to have a per-user configuration. In this case, the software installer writes to areas of the registry and file system available to the current user only and makes its program shortcuts available only to the current user.

For an older program that requires a per-user configuration, you can make the program available to multiple users by completing the following steps:

1. Log on to the computer using an account that should have access to the program.

2. Install the software using its Setup program.

3. Repeat this process for each user that requires the program.

For a newer program that doesn't require a per-user configuration but was installed only for a particular user, you can make the program available to all users on your computer by completing the following steps:

1. While logged on as the user who installed the program, click the Start menu, right-click All Programs, and then click Open.

2. Open the Programs folder and right-click the folder for the program group or the shortcut you want to work with. Then select Copy or Cut from the shortcut menu.

3. Click the Start menu, right-click All Programs, and then click Open All Users.

4. Open the Programs folder, right-click an open space, and then select Paste. The program group or shortcut should now be available to all users of the computer.

5. Repeat these steps as necessary to copy all the related program groups and shortcuts for the program.

TIP If you plan on using Windows XP Mode, remember this technique. In Windows XP Mode, the list of Windows XP applications that you can launch from the Start menu of Windows 7 is drawn from applications that have been installed for all users. Because Windows XP Mode is used for troublesome programs, it's not unusual to find that one of these programs is installed for the logged-on user only rather than for all users, and you'll need to fix this by using a similar technique while working within the virtual environment.

Sometimes you'll want a program to be available only to you rather than to all users of your computer. If so, complete the following steps to modify the way the programs works:

1. While logged on to your user account, click the Start menu, right-click All Programs, and then click Open All Users.

2. In the Programs folder, right-click the folder for the program group or shortcut that you want to work with, and select Cut.

3. Click the Start menu, right-click All Programs, and then click Open.

4. In the Programs folder, right-click an open space, and then select Paste. The program group or shortcut should now be available only to the currently logged-on user.

5. Repeat these steps as necessary to copy all the related program groups and shortcuts for the software application.

NOTE Moving the software's program group or shortcuts doesn't prevent other users from running the program—it simply hides the program from other users. They may still be able to start the software from Windows Explorer.

Using Windows XP Mode

Windows XP Mode provides additional application compatibility by allowing you to run older software in a virtual Windows XP environment from your Windows 7 desktop. After you set up the virtual environment and install programs in it, the programs can be seen and accessed from the Start menu in Windows 7.

Whether your computer is running a 32-bit or 64-bit version of Windows 7, the virtual environment will simulate 32-bit Windows XP. Generally, this is what you want because it allows you to run 16-bit and MS-DOS programs as well as 32-bit programs that might not run reliably otherwise.

Windows XP Mode requires virtualization software such as Windows Virtual PC and works only with Windows 7 Home Premium and higher versions. Both Windows XP Mode and Windows Virtual PC are available for free on the Microsoft website. To download Windows XP Mode and the required software, visit the Windows Virtual PC website (*http://www.microsoft.com/windows/virtual-pc/download.aspx*).

The basic steps for installation are:

1. On the Virtual PC download page, select whether you are running 32-bit or 64-bit Windows 7, and then select the display language for Windows XP Mode, such as English.

2. Click the link provided to download Windows XP Mode. Double-click the download to begin installation, and then follow the prompts.

3. Click the link provided to download Windows Virtual PC. Double-click the download to begin installation, and then follow the prompts.

4. If needed, download and apply the update for Windows XP Mode.

Microsoft has added features to Windows Virtual PC to make it easy to run many older Windows XP applications in Windows 7. You'll find it is fairly easy to set up Window XP Mode and install programs in it. Afterward, you can run Windows XP Mode applications with one click from the Windows 7 Start menu.

Resolving Compatibility Issues

Windows 7 warns you when you try to install a program with a known compatibility issue, and then it starts the Program Compatibility Assistant to help you resolve the problem. You can also manually start the assistant if a program won't install or run as you want it to.

The Program Compatibility Assistant is a multiple-page wizard. Whether Windows starts the assistant or you do, the basic and advanced techniques for troubleshooting are the same. You can manually start basic troubleshooting by locating the program file or program shortcut in Windows Explorer or on the desktop, right-clicking it, and then selecting Troubleshoot Compatibility. Upon starting, the assistant tries to detect compatibility issues. If the assistant detects compatibility issues, you can run the program using its recommended fixes, as shown in Figure 5-4.

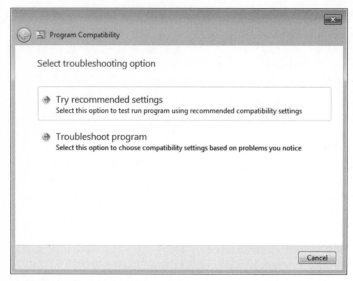

FIGURE 5-4 Resolving compatibility issues

To proceed, simply click Try Recommended Settings, review the settings or compatibility mode that will be applied, and then click Start The Program. After running the program, you'll need to continue through the wizard. Click Next, and then do one of the following:

- Click Yes, Save These Settings For This Program if the compatibility settings resolved the problem and you want to keep the settings.

- Click No, Try Again Using Different Settings if the compatibility settings didn't resolve the problem and you want to repeat this testing process from the beginning.

- Click No, Report The Problem To Microsoft And Check Online For A Solution if the compatibility settings didn't resolve the problem and you'd like to check for a possible solution online.

- Click Cancel if you want to discard the compatibility settings and exit the wizard.

TIP You can also initiate troubleshooting by using program shortcuts on the Start menu. To do this, however, you may need to hold Shift before right-clicking the program's shortcut and then selecting Troubleshoot Compatibility.

Basic troubleshooting works most of the time, but sometimes you'll need to dig a little deeper to resolve a compatibility issue. You can do this by following these steps:

1. Restart the Program Compatibility Assistant using the technique discussed previously. After the assistant completes its initial check of the program, click Troubleshoot Program.

2. On the What Problems Do You Notice? page, select options corresponding to the problems you've seen. The selections you make determine the wizard pages you see when you click Next and continue troubleshooting.

When you select The Program Worked On Earlier Versions Of Windows But Won't Install Or Run Now, you are prompted to specify which version of Windows the program worked on previously, such as Windows XP Service Pack 2 or Windows 98. Your choice sets the compatibility mode, so choose the operating system for which the program was designed. When running the program, Windows 7 simulates the environment for this operating system.

> **REAL WORLD** If you have the original media for the program, the disc or the box it came in should tell you what version of Windows the program was designed for. As compatibility is specific to both the Windows version and service pack versions, pay particular attention to any service pack listed as supported as well.

When you select The Program Opens But Doesn't Display Correctly, you must next choose the type of display problem you are seeing. Your selections restrict the video display using 256 colors, 640 × 480 screen resolution, or both to help with programs that have problems running at higher screen resolutions and color depths. Your selections can also disable themes, desktop compositing, and display scaling of high dpi settings.

> **REAL WORLD** Display problems are common with games and educational software that require specific display settings. For software designed for Windows 98 or earlier, using 256 colors, 640 × 480 screen resolution, or both can sometimes resolve a problem. With new programs, however, you might introduce new problems by selecting 256 colors or 640 × 480 screen resolution; in this case, try disabling themes, desktop compositing, and display scaling to resolve your problem.

When you choose The Program Requires Additional Permissions, the program will be configured to run with administrator privileges. Many programs developed for Windows XP and earlier versions of Windows need to run with elevated privileges to function properly. The program will then always attempt to run elevated privileges and prompt you for permission or consent as appropriate.

When you choose I Don't See My Problem Listed, the wizard will behave as if you had selected all three of the previous options. You can specify the version of Windows the program worked on previously, indicate any display problems you noticed, and specify that the program requires additional permissions.

After you work your way through the assistant, review the compatibility settings that will be applied. If you want to test your settings, click Start The Program. The assistant will run the program with the chosen compatibility settings. After Windows runs the program, go back to the assistant, click Next, and then do one of the following:

- Click Yes, Save These Settings For This Program if the compatibility settings resolved the problem and you want to keep the settings.

- Click No, Try Again Using Different Settings if the compatibility settings didn't resolve the problem and you want to repeat this testing process from the beginning.

- Click No, Report The Problem To Microsoft And Check Online For A Solution if the compatibility settings didn't resolve the problem and you'd like to check for a possible solution online.

- Click Cancel if you want to discard the compatibility settings and exit the wizard.

TIP Don't worry if your computer's display settings are reset during this process. You can restore the original display settings simply by exiting the program that is running in compatibility mode.

If you still have problems running a program, you might need to modify the compatibility settings again. You can also contact the software developer for an updated version or try running the program in Windows XP Mode.

Managing Installed Software

After you install software, you'll sometimes need to make configuration changes to your computer or the software. Although most programs register file types so that you can double-click related files to open them in the program, you may need to customize this process to change which files are opened in one program or another. You may need to reconfigure and repair software that isn't working properly. Or you may need to uninstall a program that you no longer need or use.

Choosing Default Programs

Many programs that you install have associated file types. Because of this, the installation process may configure your computer to open certain files in the program automatically when you click or double-click them in Windows Explorer. The installation process may also configure your computer so that when you insert media containing music, video, or pictures, the media is opened and played automatically using the program.

Associating a program with particular file types and running a program automatically with certain types of media are separate features. You make files with a specific file extension or type open in a specific program by associating the file extension or type with the program. You make media on CDs, DVDs, or portable devices open and play in a particular program by making a program the default for AutoPlay. AutoPlay was discussed previously in the "Understanding Autorun and Tweaking AutoPlay" section.

You manage file associations and default programs in several ways. You can:

- Set global defaults for all users of your computer.
- Set defaults for file types used with a particular program.
- Set defaults for individual file types.

You use global and program defaults to control many file associations at once. Global defaults control which web browser, email program, media player, and Java Virtual Machine are used by default by all users of your computer. You configure global defaults by completing the following steps:

1. Log on to your computer using an account with administrator privileges.

2. Click Start, and then click Default Programs. Or click Start, type **default programs**, and then press Enter.

3. Click Set Program Access And Computer Defaults, and then choose a configuration from one of the following options:

   - **Computer Manufacturer**   Restores the manufacturer's original defaults for web browsing, sending and receiving email, playing media files, instant messaging, and Java Virtual Machine support, as well as whether you have access to other programs (only if your computer came preinstalled with a customized version of Windows).

   - **Microsoft Windows**   Specifies that the currently installed Microsoft Windows programs are the defaults for web browsing, sending and receiving email, playing media files, instant messaging, and Java Virtual Machine support.

   - **Non-Microsoft**   Specifies the currently installed non–Microsoft Windows programs as the defaults for web browsing, sending and receiving email, playing media files, instant messaging, and Java Virtual Machine support.

   - **Custom**   Allows you to choose programs as the defaults for web browsing, sending and receiving email, playing media files, instant messaging, and Java Virtual Machine support. Each program available to use as a default has a related Enable Access To This Program check box. If you clear this check box, you remove access to the program when a viable alternative is installed.

4. Click OK to save your settings.

Default settings for programs allow you to specify which file types open in which programs automatically, and they always override global default settings. You can configure individual defaults only for the currently logged on user. As an example, you might want Windows Media Player to be your default audio player, but the global default for all users could be set to use Windows Media Center.

You can configure your default programs by completing the following steps:

1. Click Start, and then click Default Programs. Or click Start, type **default programs**, and then press Enter.

2. Click Set Your Default Programs, and then select the program you want to work with in the Programs list (see Figure 5-5).

3. If you want the program to be the default for all the file types and protocols it supports, click Set This Program As Default and click OK. Skip the remaining steps.

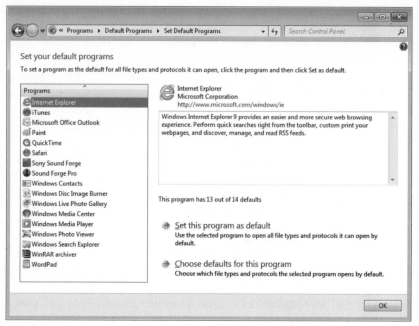

FIGURE 5-5 Configuring default programs

4. If you want the program to be the default for specific file types and protocols, click Choose Defaults For This Program.

5. Select the file extensions and protocols for which the program should be the default, and then click Save. Repeat this process as necessary to configure other default programs.

You use defaults for individual file extensions and file types to fine-tune file associations. For example, you may have configured all image files to open in a particular program but want .JPG image files to open in another program. By modifying the file association for .JPG files, you can easily configure this.

To associate a file type or protocol with a specific program, complete the following steps:

1. Click Start, and then click Default Programs. Or click Start, type **default programs**, and then press Enter.

2. Click Associate A File Type Or Protocol With A Program. On the Set Associations page, current file associations are listed by file extension and the current default for that extension. To change the file association for an extension, click the file extension, and then click Change Program.

3. The Recommended Programs list shows programs that are registered in the operating system as supporting files with the selected extension. Click a recommended program to set it as the default for the selected extension, and then click OK.

4. The Other Programs list shows programs that might also support the selected extension. Click a program to set it as the default for the selected extension, and then click OK. Or click Browse to locate another program to use as the default.

Reconfiguring, Repairing, and Uninstalling Software

You manage installed software by using the Programs And Features page in Control Panel. You use the Programs And Features page to reconfigure, repair, or uninstall software by following these steps:

1. Click Start, type **appwiz.cpl**, and then press Enter.
2. In the Name list, click the program you want to work with.
3. On the toolbar, select one of the following options:
   - Change, to modify the program's configuration
   - Repair, to repair the program's installation
   - Uninstall, to uninstall the program
   - Uninstall/Change, to uninstall or change a program with an older installer program

Sometimes the uninstall process will fail. If this happens, you may be able to resolve the problem simply by rerunning the Uninstaller for the program. Occasionally, you may need to clean up the registry and program files after a failed uninstall. A program called the Windows Installer Cleanup utility can help you clean up the registry. You'll find more information about the utility and the software for downloading online at the Microsoft Support website (*http://support.microsoft.com/kb/290301*).

The operating system allows you to remove programs that were installed with Windows-compatible setup programs. Programs designed for Windows 2000 and earlier may have a separate Uninstall utility. Some older programs work by copying their data files to a program folder, and you uninstall these programs simply by deleting the related folder.

After you uninstall a program, check the Program Files folder and other locations for data left behind, either inadvertently or by design. Before deleting any remaining data, you should determine whether the files contain important data or custom settings that could be used again if you reinstall the program.

Because Windows components are features that are turned on or off, you sometimes can repair problems with a Windows component by turning it off and then turning it back on by following these steps:

1. Click Start, type **optionalfeatures.exe**, and then press Enter.
2. When you clear the feature check box and then click OK, Windows 7 reconfigures components as appropriate for any changes you've made. You may need to restart your computer. If prompted to do so, save your work and then click Restart.

3. Click Start, type **optionalfeatures.exe**, and then press Enter.

4. When you reselect the feature check box and click OK, Windows 7 reinstalls the feature.

Viewing and Managing Running Programs

You can view information related to running programs by using Task Manager. You start Task Manager by pressing Ctrl+Shift+Esc, or by pressing Ctrl+Alt+Delete and selecting Start Task Manager.

Task Manager, shown in Figure 5-6, can also help you manage currently running programs and processes. For example, if a program is not responding and you want to quit the program, you can use Task Manager to force the program to stop running and exit.

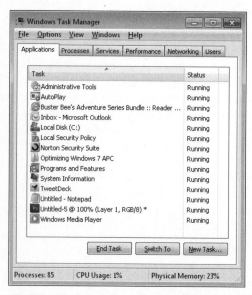

FIGURE 5-6 Viewing running applications in Windows Task Manager

In Task Manager, you use the Applications and Processes tabs to work with running programs. Applications lists applications you are currently running by name and status, such as Running or Not Responding. To exit a program, click the program in the Task list and then click End Task.

Processes lists all programs and processes you are running on the computer by image name, your user name, and resource usage. To stop a process, click the process and then click End Process. You can also right-click a process and select from an extended list of management options, including:

Create Dump File   Creates a memory dump file for the selected process

End Process Tree   Stops the process and all dependent processes

Open File Location   Opens the folder containing the executable file for the process in Windows Explorer

Properties   Opens the Properties dialog box for the executable file

UAC Virtualization   Allows you to modify UAC virtualization settings as necessary for debugging

By default, the Task Manager Processes tab shows only the running processes for the currently logged-on user. To see running processes for all users, click Show Processes From All Users and provide consent or credentials if prompted. You'll then see all processes running on your computer.

CHAPTER 6

Tracking System Performance and Health

Your computer's performance levels are directly related to its health. Whether you have a desktop, laptop, or tablet PC, your computer was designed to be paused (by putting it in sleep mode) and resumed. All that pausing and resuming can have unintended consequences on the overall performance of your computer, especially after days or weeks of pause and resume. So the first thing I ask anyone experiencing a problem with a personal computer is this: When was the last time you shut down and then restarted your computer?

Beyond a simple restart, there are three things you need to know to understand issues that can affect your computer's performance. You need to understand your computer's baseline performance levels—the best indicator of this is the Windows Experience Index. You need to determine what is currently happening on your computer in terms of running applications, processes, and services—Task Manager makes this easy. And you need to know what problems (if any) your computer is experiencing—the best way to track problems is to examine the event logs.

Tracking Relative Performance

During installation, Windows 7 assigned your computer a Windows Experience Index. This index is a relative rating of your computer's performance capabilities with regard to its hardware configuration. It's relative because your computer's actual performance depends on many factors, including whether you've followed the tips and techniques discussed in this book to squeeze every last bit of power out of your computer while making the most of the included features and options.

Understanding Your Computer's Relative Performance Levels

To assign the index, Windows 7 examines your computer's processor, physical memory (RAM), graphics card, and primary hard disk:

- **Processor**   The number of calculations per second that your computer's processor can perform as related to the number of processors/processor cores installed and the processor type

- **Memory (RAM)**   The number of memory operations per second that your computer's memory can perform as related to the total amount of physical memory installed

- **Graphics**   The relative performance of your computer's graphics adapter when supporting Windows Aero

- **Gaming Graphics**   The relative performance of your computer's graphics adapter for multimedia as related to the total amount of graphics memory installed

- **Primary Hard Disk**   The data transfer rate of your computer's primary hard disk as related to read/write performance

Each of these areas is scored on a scale of 1.0 to 7.9. You can view your computer's Windows Experience Index and the related subscores by clicking Start, typing **Performance Information**, and then pressing Enter. As shown in Figure 6-1, the Performance Information And Tools page lists your computer's performance scores by component. If for some reason the assessment hasn't run, you can run an assessment by clicking the link provided. You also can re-run the assessment at any time by clicking the Re-run The Assessment link.

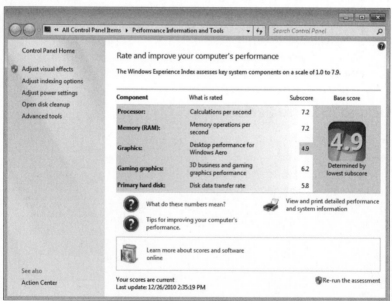

FIGURE 6-1 Checking your computer's relative performance

NOTE Some open and running applications can affect your subscores, as can certain background housekeeping tasks. If you suspect that your computer's subscores are inaccurate, close open applications, stop background tasks, and rerun the assessment. Note also that Microsoft states that it may update the scoring engine from time to time to accommodate advances in computer technology, and such an update might reduce certain subscores.

The lowest subscore determines the base score, because this component represents your computer's performance bottleneck. Although your computer's base score is determined by the lowest subscore, a selective average of the subscores often can be more meaningful. I calculate the selective average by adding all the values except for the primary hard disk and dividing by 4.

REAL WORLD If your computer's primary hard disk has a subscore of 3.8 or less, the hard disk probably doesn't support caching and you should strongly consider replacing the hard disk with a newer, better hard disk. Other than that, most current computers have a primary hard disk that uses caching and operates at either 5400 rpm or 7200 rpm, and as long as the hard disk is functioning and not full, its performance rating is likely to be 3.9 or greater. An application that constantly reads from disk will be relatively slow no matter what, as will an application that constantly writes to disk. For a personal computer, the only real fix for relatively poor read/write performance is a solid state drive and a hard disk controller that knows how to operate with this type of drive.

If your computer's primary hard disk has a subscore greater than 3.8, I think you'll find that the selective average score better determines the type of programs you can run and the types of tasks you can perform. In the example, the computer's subscore is 4.9, but the selective average score of 6.4 is a better indicator of the overall user experience.

Table 6-1 discusses what the selective average score means to you as far as your computer's performance. You can improve your computer's scores and relative performance levels by upgrading the hardware components responsible for the lowest scores. For example, if memory is your lowest score, you could add memory to improve your rating. If graphics and gaming graphics are your lowest scores, you could upgrade the graphic card to improve your rating.

TABLE 6-1 What Your Computer's Selective Score Means

SELECTIVE AVERAGE SCORE	YOUR USER EXPERIENCE	WHAT THE SCORE MEANS
1.0 to 1.9	Extremely poor	This computer is outdated but can be used for word processing, web browsing, and email messaging. The computer will be severely limited and very slow.

SELECTIVE AVERAGE SCORE	YOUR USER EXPERIENCE	WHAT THE SCORE MEANS
2.0 to 2.9	Less than optimal	This computer is okay for general computing tasks, such as word processing, email messaging, and web browsing. Business applications, basic gaming, and basic multimedia may run but won't perform well overall. The user experience will be less than optimal.
3.0 to 3.9	Okay	This computer is okay for general computing, business applications, gaming, and multimedia. The computer probably isn't suited for advanced gaming or advanced multimedia. The user experience should be okay.
4.0 to 4.9	Good	This computer is good for most computing tasks, including advanced business applications, advanced gaming, and advanced multimedia. The user experience should be relatively good.
5.0 to 5.9	Superior	This computer is superior for most computing tasks, even for demanding tasks that are both graphics-intensive and processor-intensive. The user experience should be very good.
6.0 to 6.9	Outstanding	This computer is outstanding for most computing tasks, even for 3D graphics and 3D applications that are both graphics-intensive and processor-intensive. The user experience should be outstanding.

SELECTIVE AVERAGE SCORE	YOUR USER EXPERIENCE	WHAT THE SCORE MEANS
7.0 to 7.9	Excellent	This computer is excellent for most computing tasks, including 3D graphics and 3D applications that are both highly graphics-intensive and highly processor-intensive. The user experience should be excellent.

Your computer probably has a base score of between 3.0 and 5.9. If your computer scores in the 6s and 7s, it's a powerhouse at the top end of the scale. Part of the graphics subscore relates to whether your computer supports Windows Aero. The Aero interface provides animated window closing and opening, live thumbnail previews, smoother window dragging, and transparent window frames. To use Aero, your computer's graphics card must support the Windows Display Driver Model (WDDM) and DirectX 9.0 or later—this is what you should focus on.

WDDM 1.0 and DirectX 9.0 were both released around the same time as Windows Vista. For Windows 7, display drivers that support WDDM 1.1 or later offer improved performance while also reducing the per-window memory usage by up to 50 percent. WDDM 1.1 also supports DirectX 11, which enables a computer's graphics processing unit (GPU) to more efficiently work with multiple cores and greatly improves graphics handling for all types of display rendering.

Improving Your Computer's Relative Performance Levels

On the Performance Information And Tools page, you can get more detailed information about your computer's configuration by clicking View And Print Detailed Performance And System Information. As shown in Figure 6-2, the details page provides information on:

- **System**   Lists the model and manufacturer of your computer as well as the system memory and system type. Also provides an easy way to verify the number of processor cores.

- **Storage**   Lists the total capacity of all storage, individual disk partitions, and media drives. Details on total partition size and free space is also shown. Similar information is provided in the Computer window, but the Computer window doesn't add up your total storage space.

- **Graphics**   Lists the model and type of your computer's display adapter, the display adapter driver version, the supported DirectX version, and the current resolution setting for your computer's monitors. Also lists details about graphics memory, which is different from standard memory.

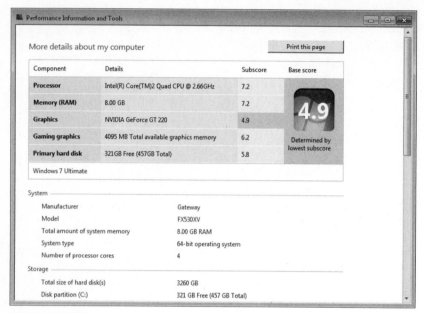

Component	Details	Subscore	Base score
Processor	Intel(R) Core(TM)2 Quad CPU @ 2.66GHz	7.2	
Memory (RAM)	8.00 GB	7.2	
Graphics	NVIDIA GeForce GT 220	4.9	**4.9**
Gaming graphics	4095 MB Total available graphics memory	6.2	Determined by lowest subscore
Primary hard disk	321GB Free (457GB Total)	5.8	

Windows 7 Ultimate

System

Manufacturer	Gateway
Model	FX530XV
Total amount of system memory	8.00 GB RAM
System type	64-bit operating system
Number of processor cores	4

Storage

Total size of hard disk(s)	3260 GB
Disk partition (C:)	321 GB Free (457 GB Total)

FIGURE 6-2 Checking your computer's configuration details

- **Network** Lists the model and type of your computer's display network adapter.

NOTE While you are viewing the detailed information, click Print This Page to print this information for future reference.

Clearly, your computer's system type, processor, and RAM have a big impact on overall performance. If your computer has an older or single-core processor, you may be able to boost performance dramatically by upgrading the processor, especially if your computer's processor subscore is 4.5 or less. However, performing a processor upgrade isn't the easiest thing to do. Many things can go wrong, and your older computer probably won't be able to use the latest processors anyway. At best, you might be able to upgrade to a similar class CPU that is only marginally faster; so instead of trying to upgrade the processor, I recommend:

- Determining whether your current processor supports 64-bit computing. If you have an older computer that was upgraded to 32-bit Windows 7, you might be able to install 64-bit Windows 7. Since Windows 7 ships with both 32-bit and 64-bit media, you get a performance boost at no upfront cost (although you will need to fully reinstall Windows 7 and your programs). See "How 64-bit Software Works" in Chapter 5 for more information.

- Determining whether you can add more RAM to your computer. If your computer has less than 8 GB of RAM, you may be able to improve performance by installing more memory. Remember, the memory must operate at a speed compatible with your computer's motherboard and system bus, and you can't mix and match different types of memory. Often, you'll have the best chances for success if you remove your existing memory and replace it with the new memory.

Your computer's primary hard disk also has a big impact on overall performance. The primary hard disk is the one most used by the operating system and programs. If you have an older computer and its primary drive has a low performance subscore, you may see a significant reduction in boot and wake from sleep times by upgrading the primary hard disk to a newer model that is faster and supports caching. However, moving your primary disk isn't very easy; these two tricks will save you a lot of time and heartache:

- Try moving your computer's paging file to a faster, newer disk, as discussed in "Fine-Tuning Virtual Memory" in Chapter 8.
- Try using Windows ReadyBoost to shift some of your computer's system cache reads and writes to faster flash memory. See "Enhancing Performance with ReadyBoost" in Chapter 8.

If your computer's primary drive has a relatively good performance subscore, you can maintain relatively good disk performance by:

- Running a full check disk on your primary hard drive at least once a year. Be sure to perform error repair and bad sector recovery as well.
- Defragmenting your primary hard drive at least once a year. Although you can defragment other drives, fragmentation of the primary hard drive is what most affects performance.
- Cleaning up your primary hard drive at least once every other month and always ensuring that your primary drive has at least 15 percent of its disk space free.

NOTE DiskCleanup and other disk utilities are discussed in Chapter 8.

Graphics memory can also affect relative performance levels. Look at:

- **Shared system memory** A reflection of physical memory (RAM) that is shared between the graphics card and the CPU. Shared memory used by the graphics card leaves less physical memory available for applications and the operating system.
- **Dedicated graphics memory** A reflection of the actual memory on its graphics card or cards. If your computer has no or low dedicated graphics memory, installing a new graphics card with 512 MB or more of dedicated RAM would substantially increase relative performance levels.
- **Total available graphics memory** A combination of shared memory and dedicated memory. If your computer has 1 GB of dedicated graphics memory and 3 GB of shared graphics memory, it has 4 GB of total available memory for graphics.

Following this, if your computer has 4 GB of RAM, and 3 GB of that currently is being used by the graphics card to perform graphics rendering for a graphic-intensive application or program, only 1 GB is available for other uses. In this case, you'd have a better experience if you added RAM, upgraded to a graphics card with 1 GB or higher of dedicated memory, or both.

As a final note, remember that the performance subscores are meant to be helpful guidelines. You can squeeze extra performance out of your computer by using the techniques I've discussed here, as well as other techniques I've discussed previously. For example, if your computer has a low score in graphics, gaming graphics, or both, you can improve overall performance by turning off graphics-intensive features of the operating system, as discussed in "Optimizing Interface Performance" in Chapter 1.

Checking Current Performance Levels

"Viewing and Managing Running Programs" in Chapter 5 discussed basic techniques for working with Task Manager. Now let's take a closer look. Start Task Manager by pressing Ctrl+Shift+Esc. The Applications tab shows the status of currently running programs. You can switch to an application and make it active by selecting the application and then clicking Switch To, and you can start a new program by clicking New Task and then entering a command to run the application.

When you start an application or run a command, Windows 7 starts one or more processes to handle the related program. Processes that you start are called interactive processes. If an application is active and selected, the interactive process has control over the keyboard and mouse until you switch control by terminating the program or selecting a different application. When an application's process has control, it's said to be running in the foreground.

Tracking Applications and Processes

Processes can also run in the background. For processes you started, this means that programs that aren't currently active can continue to operate; however, they generally aren't given the same priority as active processes. Windows also has background processes that run independently of your user session. These processes are related to startup applications, scheduled tasks, housekeeping activities, and so on.

The Processes tab in Task Manager, shown in Figure 6-3, provides detailed information about running processes. Select Show Processes From All Users to view all processes that are running, including those from the operating system, local services, the interactive user logged on to the local console (you), and remote users. If your computer isn't responding well, you can use this information to determine which processes are overconsuming system resources. The default columns are:

- **Image Name** Specifies the name of the process or the related executable
- **User Name** Specifies the name of the user or system service running the process

- **CPU**   Specifies the percentage of CPU utilization for the process
- **Memory (Private Working Set)**   Specifies the amount of memory the process is currently using
- **Description**   Provides a description or proper name of the process

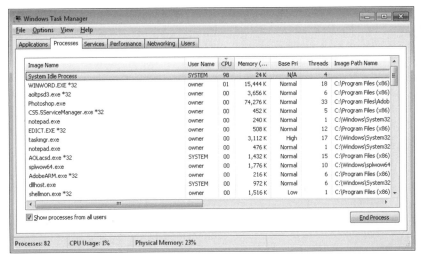

FIGURE 6-3 Tracking resource usage by processes

To get even more information, you can add columns to the Processes tab. Click View and choose Select Columns. Use the dialog box provided to select the columns to add. For troubleshooting performance and related issues, you might want to add these columns:

- **Base Priority**   Indicates the priority of the process, relative to other running processes. When there is resource contention between a higher-priority process and a lower-priority process, the higher-priority process will be given more resources relative to the lower-priority process. The priorities from lowest to highest are: Low, Below Normal, Normal, Above Normal, High, and RealTime. Most processes have a Normal priority by default.
- **CPU Time**   Shows the total CPU cycle time used by a process since it was started. If you want to see the processes that are using the most CPU time, display this column and then click the column header to sort process entries by CPU time.
- **Handles**   Shows the current number of file handles maintained by the process. Use the handle count to gauge how dependent the process is on the file system. Each file handle requires system memory to be maintained.
- **I/O Reads, I/O Writes**   Shows the total number of disk input/output (I/O) reads or writes since the process was started. Together, the number of I/O reads and writes tells you how much disk I/O activity is related to the process.

- **Page Faults** Shows the number of page faults actively occurring because of the process. A page fault occurs when a process requests a page in memory and Windows can't find the page at the requested location. If the requested page is elsewhere in memory, the fault is called a soft page fault. If the requested page must be retrieved from disk, the fault is called a hard page fault. Hard faults can cause significant delays, but most processors can handle a large number of soft faults.

- **Paged Pool, Nonpaged Pool** Shows paged pool and nonpaged pool memory usage, respectively. Paged pool is an area of system memory for objects that can be written to disk when they aren't used. Nonpaged pool is an area of system memory for objects that can't be written to disk. Processes that require a large amount of nonpaged pool memory can affect performance, especially when they are vying for resources with other processes.

- **Peak Working Set** Shows the highest amount of memory used by the process. The difference between current memory usage and peak memory usage is important to note; some applications use a lot of memory when performing certain tasks, which can degrade performance when they are vying for resources with other processes.

- **Threads** Shows the current number of threads that the process is using. Most modern applications are multithreaded. Multithreading allows concurrent execution of process requests. Some applications can dynamically control the number of concurrently executing threads to improve application performance, but too many threads can actually reduce performance because the operating system has to switch thread contexts too frequently.

Pay particular attention to the System Idle Process. This process tracks the amount of system resources that aren't being used. Thus, a 99 in the CPU column of the System Idle Process means that 99 percent of system resources currently aren't being used. Also remember that a single application can start multiple processes. To be sure you are tracking or managing the right process for an application, right-click the application on the Applications tab and select Go To Process.

To stop an application, you'll usually want to target the main application process as well as dependent processes, either by right-clicking the application on the Applications tab and then clicking End Task or by right-clicking the main application process on the Processes tab and then clicking End Process. You can also right-click the main process or a dependent process on the Processes tab, and then select End Process Tree.

Tracking Performance and Resource Usage

All running processes, whether operating actively or in the background, affect the performance of your computer. At times, your computer may seem less responsive than usual and you may want to try to determine why. The Performance tab in Task Manager provides a quick way to check system resource usage and relative performance levels.

Several CPU and memory usage graphs are provided to help you understand how resources are being used. The CPU Usage graph shows the current percentage of processor usage. The CPU Usage History graph shows processor usage plotted over time, and the Update Speed setting, on the View menu, determines how often the graph is updated. If your computer has multiple CPUs, you'll see one graph for each CPU by default.

Figure 6-4 shows the CPU and memory usage for a computer with four CPU cores under normal usage conditions. This computer's CPU cores are operating normally and are not heavily taxed. The few peaks shown are not remarkable; they probably occurred when applications were opened or new tasks were started. The memory usage levels are also normal and not remarkable.

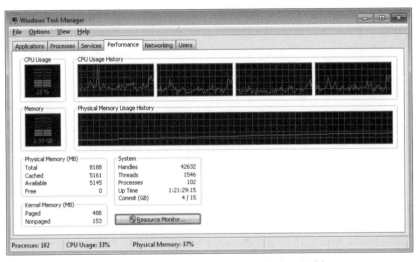

FIGURE 6-4 Tracking processor and memory usage under normal usage conditions

Contrast this to the CPU and memory usage for the same computer shown in Figure 6-5. In this case, the computer is experiencing periods of high CPU usage. The continuing peaks and high usage levels in this instance are remarkable, especially if they represent normal usage conditions. However, this computer doesn't have a performance problem related to its CPUs. Rather, it is simply performing CPU-intensive operations, and those operations are ongoing.

NOTE You can view a close-up of the CPU graphs by double-clicking in the Performance tab. Double-clicking again returns you to normal viewing mode.

TIP Don't overlook the status panel at the bottom of the tab. This panel shows the total number of running processes, the percentage of CPU usage, and the percentage of physical memory usage.

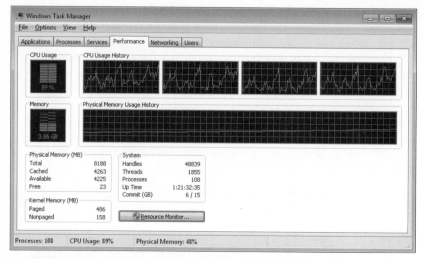

FIGURE 6-5 Tracking processor and memory usage under high usage conditions

However, if CPU usage were consistently and continually high on all CPUs, you would want to examine running applications and their processes to get a better understanding of what is happening on the computer. You might, for example, be running processor-intensive applications, or you simply might need to consider upgrading your computer's CPUs to perform the kinds of tasks you want to perform.

Memory is often a source of performance problems. The Performance tab's Memory graph shows the amount of physical memory currently being used by the computer, graphed to reflect the percentage of total memory. The Physical Memory Usage History graph shows physical memory usage plotted over time. If your computer is consistently low on available memory, you might want to consider tuning or adding memory.

The computer shown in the examples doesn't have a memory issue. In the second example, the computer is using 3.86 GB of memory and still has more than 4.22 GB of available memory. But if memory usage were considerably and consistently higher in this case, you would want to examine running processes and take a closer look at what was happening on the computer. For example, applications running in the background, such as a virus checker or backup software, might be using memory resources, or you simply might need to consider upgrading your computer's CPUs to perform the kinds of tasks you want to perform.

In addition to the graphs on the Performance tab, you'll find these statistics related to memory usage, with all the values in megabytes (MB):

- **Total Physical Memory**   Displays the amount of physical RAM on your computer. This doesn't include graphics memory or virtual memory.

- **Cached Physical Memory** Displays the amount of memory marked as "in use" for system caching. This essentially is the amount of memory currently reserved for when a process needs it.
- **Available Physical Memory** Displays the amount of RAM available for use by processes.
- **Free Physical Memory** Displays the amount of RAM not being used or cached. This is usually a relatively small number because Windows 7 tries to cache memory as much as possible to be able to allocate it quickly to processes.
- **Kernel Memory Paged** Shows the amount of non-critical kernel memory that is paged to virtual memory.
- **Kernel Memory Nonpaged** Shows the amount of critical kernel memory that is resident in physical memory.

REAL WORLD Critical portions of kernel memory used by the operating system must operate in physical RAM and can't be paged to virtual memory. The rest of kernel memory can be paged to virtual memory.

Under the System heading are statistics related to the total number of handles, threads, and processes, as well as total up time of the computer since it was last started. In the example, the computer is quite active, with 48,839 open handles, 1855 active threads, and 108 running processes. Of particular note is the Commit value. Here the Commit value is shown in gigabytes (GB), but it could also be shown in MB.

The Commit value shows the virtual memory currently in use followed by the total amount of virtual memory available. This is important because virtual memory is memory stored on disk in one or more paging files. If the current page file usage, reflected by current virtual memory usage, is consistently close to the maximum value, you might want to add physical memory, increase the amount of virtual memory, or both.

With the Performance tab selected in Task Manager, you can show kernel usage by clicking Show Kernel Times on the View menu. Tracking kernel CPU usage can help you better understand how the operating system is using the CPU. Usage by the kernel is plotted in red and reflects total usage.

Event Logging and Viewing

Windows 7 stores warnings, errors, and other information generated for tracking purposes in the event logs. There two general types of event logs. Windows logs are a type of log file that the operating system uses to record general system events related to applications, security, setup, and system components. Applications and services logs are a type of log file that specific applications and services use to record application-specific or service-specific events.

Digging into the Event Logs

Event logs use a proprietary format that is readable only in the Event Viewer utility, which can be accessed by clicking Start, typing **eventvwr.msc**, and pressing Enter. As long as you have administrator privileges on your computer, you can access the event logs and use them to track system health and system security issues.

The Windows logs that you should track closely are:

- **Application**   Records events logged by applications, such as an error that results in a system fault

- **Security**   Records events configured for auditing, including user logon and logoff

- **Setup**   Records events logged by the operating system during setup, as well as whenever the installed state of components change, such as when you apply an update or service pack to the operating system

- **System**   Records events logged by the operating system, its services, and its components—especially state changes and failures to load or start

If you are experiencing a problem with a specific application or service, you can check for a related applications and services log. For example, you can use the Media Center log to help you resolve issues related to Windows Media Center, or you can use the Microsoft\Windows\Audio\Operational log to examine issues related to the Windows Audio service.

In Event Viewer, you can work with your computer's event logs in the following ways:

- To view all errors and warnings for all logs, expand Custom Views and then select Administrative Events. The main page displays a list of all warning and error events for the server.

- To view events in a specific log, expand the Windows Logs node, the Applications And Services Logs node, or both. Select the log you want to view, such as Application.

While you are working with a particular event log, use the information in the Source column to determine which component logged a particular event. In the example shown in Figure 6-6, the computer's DNS client is the source of the event.

The logged details for an event provide a quick overview of when, where, and how an event occurred. The event level tells you the seriousness of the event. An informational event is usually related to a successful action. A warning event tells you about a less serious (and often only temporarily) problem that occurred, such as an error detected on a disk device during paging. An error event tells you about a more serious but noncritical problem that occurred, such as a write failure to a disk device. A critical event tells you about a serious problem for which there is no recovery.

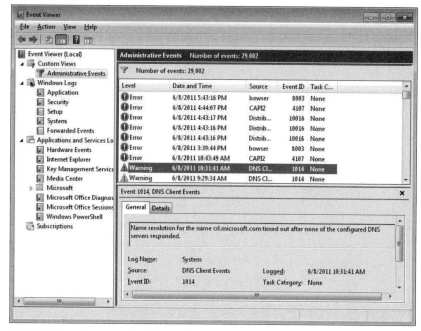

FIGURE 6-6 Examining events in the Event Viewer

Resolving Performance Issues with the Logs

You'll frequently see warnings and errors, and you don't need to try to determine the cause and resolution for each and every one. However, if your computer is experiencing performance issues or other problems, you should look for warnings and errors that could possibly be related to the problem, because they can help you find a resolution to the problem. Be sure to review the detailed event information as part of your troubleshooting. Click the Event Log Online Help link if you think you need more information.

If you spend just a few minutes in the event logs, you'll see just how much information your computer tracks. Wading through all that information to find what you're looking for isn't always easy, so you may need to filter the event logs to focus in on the specific information you need.

Earlier I mentioned that when you select the Administrative Events node, you see a list of all errors and warnings for all logs. That selective view of the event logs is created using a filter, and you can create your own filters to help sort through the logs by following these steps:

1. Start Event Viewer by clicking Start, typing **eventvwr.msc**, and then pressing Enter.

2. In the left pane, right-click the Custom Views node, and then click Create Custom View.

3. Use the Logged drop-down list to select a time frame for logging events, such as the Last 24 Hours, Last 7 Days, or Last 30 Days.

4. Use the Event Level check boxes to specify the level of events to include. Usually, you'll want to look for Critical, Warning, and Error events. Select Verbose to get additional details.

5. Create a custom view for either a specific set of logs or a specific set of event sources by doing one of the following:

   ■ Use the Event Logs drop-down list to select event logs to include. Select multiple event logs by selecting their check boxes. If you select specific event logs, all other event logs are excluded.

   ■ Use the Event Sources drop-down list to select event sources to include. Select multiple event sources by selecting their check boxes. If you select specific event sources, all other event sources are excluded.

6. Optionally, use the User box to specify users that should be included.

   REAL WORLD Many events are logged with the user listed as N/A, for not applicable. Events directly related to your logon and interactions with active applications may be logged with your user name, but not always. Other events may be logged with the user as System (the local system account used for running system processes and handling system-level tasks), Local Service (the local service account, which has fewer privileges than system), or Network Service (the local network service account, which has fewer privileges than system but also has access to network resources).

7. Click OK. Type a name and description for the custom view, and then specify where to save the custom view. By default, custom views are saved under the Custom Views node. You can create a new node by clicking New Folder, entering a name for the folder, and then clicking OK.

8. Click OK to close the Save Filter To Custom View dialog box. You should now see a filtered list of events.

CHAPTER 7

Analyzing and Logging Performance

Windows 7 provides many tools to help you track performance. The previous chapter discussed ways you could track current and relative performance and provided techniques for determining resource usage using Task Manager and uncovering problems using the Event Logs. Although these tools are excellent, you might need to dig deeper to diagnose complex problems and optimize performance.

Additional tools for resolving performance issues include:

- **Action Center**   Allows you to check for problems that are affecting performance and try to find solutions using automated processes.
- **Reliability Monitor**   Allows you to analyze reliability issues that are affecting performance and determine their causes.
- **Resource Monitor**   Allows you to track resource usage on the computer. The information provided is similar to Task Manager but more detailed.
- **Performance Monitor**   Allows you to log performance data, watch resource usage over time, and determine areas that can be optimized.

Resolving Failures and Reliability Issues

Windows 7 includes an automated diagnostics framework for detecting and diagnosing many common problems with applications, hardware devices, and Windows itself. Restart Manager, Action Center, and Reliability Monitor are the core components of this framework that you'll interact with.

Windows 7 uses Restart Manager to shut down and restart applications automatically. If Windows diagnostics detects that an application has stopped responding, Restart Manager attempts to stop the application's primary process and then restart the application. Problem reports related to nonresponsive applications are logged in the Action Center, as are problem reports for other types of failures.

Checking for Problems That Are Affecting Performance

After you connect a new device, whether internally or externally, Windows 7 attempts to detect the hardware and install the device automatically. If Windows 7 detects the device but cannot install the device automatically, you may find a related solution in Action Center. Typically, Action Center opens automatically, allowing you to begin troubleshooting immediately.

Similarly, if Windows diagnostics detects a problem with a hardware device or Windows component, Windows 7 displays a Problem Reports and Solutions balloon telling you there is a problem. If you click this balloon, Windows 7 opens the Action Center, which can help you resolve the problem.

On the far-right side of the taskbar, you'll find the notification area, which also has a notification icon for Action Center. If you move your mouse pointer over the Action Center icon, a tooltip provides information about alert messages and system problems that you may want to try to resolve. Clicking this icon provides more detailed information and allows you to open Action Center. You also can open Action Center by clicking Start, typing **Action Center**, and pressing Enter.

In Action Center, you can click the Security or Maintenance heading to expand the section and view more detailed information. Expand the Security area to get more information about the status and configuration of your computer's core security components. Known problems are color-coded and listed in the Security and Maintenance panels, as shown in Figure 7-1. Red-coded issues are warnings about important problems that need your attention. Orange-coded issues are cautions about problems that you might want to review.

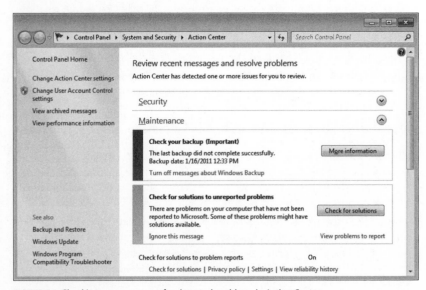

FIGURE 7-1 Checking your computer for detected problems in Action Center

Action Center notification settings control whether you are notified about problems. To view and manage these settings, click Change Action Center Settings in the left pane of Action Center. Then turn notifications for messages on or off by selecting or clearing check boxes.

Problem reporting settings control whether and how Windows checks for solutions to problems. To view and manage these settings, click Change Action Center Settings in the left pane of Action Center. Under Related Settings, click Problem Reporting Settings, and then specify when to check for solutions to problems. The default option is to automatically check for solutions. You also can elect to automatically check for solutions and send additional report data as necessary, to prompt before checking for solutions whenever a problem occurs, or to never check for solutions.

You also have the option to exclude specific programs from problem reporting. To do this, click Change Action Center Settings in the left pane of Action Center. Under Related Settings, click Problem Reporting Settings, and then click Select Programs To Exclude From Reporting. On the Advanced Problem Reporting Settings page, you can see a list of any programs that are currently excluded and add programs to this list.

Automated detection works fairly well, but some problems can be missed by the diagnostics framework. If you suspect that your computer has problems that haven't been identified, you can initiate automatic problem detection simply by opening Action Center and clicking Check For Solutions on the Maintenance panel. When this process is complete, Action Center is updated to include all newly discovered problems, and solutions are provided if known.

If automated diagnostics detects problems for which there are no solutions available, you'll see the Problem Reporting dialog box, shown in Figure 7-2. Click Send Information to send this information to Microsoft, or click Cancel to exit problem reporting without sending the information to Microsoft. If you send the information to Microsoft, the troubleshooting data is extracted to the Temp directory in your profile, sent to Microsoft, and then deleted from the Temp directory. The amount of data extracted and sent can be rather large in some instances.

FIGURE 7-2 Reporting unresolved problems to Microsoft

If automated diagnostics detects problems for which solutions are available, you can resolve the problems immediately. Each known problem will have a solution button. Click the View Problem Response button to display a page providing more information about the problem. Note the following:

- When a configuration issue is causing a problem, you'll find a description of the problem and a step-by-step guide for modifying the configuration to resolve the problem.

- When a driver or software issue is causing a problem, you'll find a link to download and install the latest driver or software update.

After you resolve a problem by installing a driver or software update, you can elect to archive the problem report for future reference by selecting the Archive This Message check box before you click OK to close the More Information page.

Analyzing Reliability Issues That Are Affecting Performance

Windows 7 tracks the relative reliability of your computer in Reliability Monitor. You can use the related reports to determine how stable your computer is and what components, applications, or devices have caused problems. When you are working with Action Center, you can access reliability reports by expanding the Maintenance panel, scrolling down, and then clicking View Reliability History.

Reliability Monitor tracks changes to the computer and compares them to changes in system stability. This gives you a graphical representation of the relationship between changes in the configuration and changes in stability. By recording software installation, software removal, application failures, hardware failures, and Windows failures, and key events regarding the configuration of your computer, Reliability Monitors gives you a timeline of changes large and small and information about their effect on reliability. You can use this information to pinpoint changes that are causing stability problems. For example, if you see a sudden drop in stability, you can click a data point and then expand the related data set to find the specific event that caused the problem.

Reliability Monitor displays stability data by days or weeks. The default view is days. To view history by weeks, click the Weeks option for View By.

Your computer's stability is graphed with values ranging from 1, meaning extremely poor reliability, to 10, meaning extremely high reliability. A graph for a computer experiencing reliability problems will be similar to the one shown in Figure 7-3.

NOTE The graph has left and right scroll buttons. By scrolling left, you can see reliability data for earlier dates. You can scroll right to go to later dates.

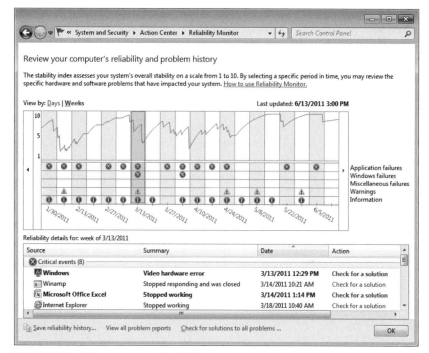

FIGURE 7-3 Checking your computer's reliability

In this example, the reliability of the computer has been severely impacted by a series of failures. Failures and other reliability events are summarized on the graph relative to the selected time period, either by day or by week. Failures are divided into three categories:

- **Application Failures**   Tracks failures caused by running applications. An application that stopped working or stopped responding is tracked as an application failure.

- **Windows Failures**   Tracks failures caused by Windows components and system hardware. A hardware error that occurred is tracked as a Windows failure, as are errors related to component configuration.

- **Miscellaneous Failures**   Tracks other types of failures that occur, such as failures caused by an unexpected shutdown of the operating system.

Reliability Monitor tags failures that have affected stability as critical. Events tagged as warnings indicate a potential to affect stability. For example, failed Windows Updates are marked as warnings because most updates need to be applied to ensure reliability and stability.

You'll also see that successful Windows updates, successful application installations, and many other system activities are logged using informational events. Although these activities don't represent failures, they do have an effect on the overall stability of your computer.

Clicking a column in the graph displays details for the events that occurred on that day or during a selected week. Events are listed by source, summary, and date. Under Action, you'll see several possible actions, depending on the type of event.

If Windows detected a critical problem and resolved it automatically, a View Problem Response link allows you to display information about how Windows resolved the problem. If the critical problem is unresolved, a Check For A Solution link lets you report the problem and check for a solution. For warnings and informational events, a View Technical Details link provides detailed technical information about the event.

The bottom panel of Reliability Monitor provides three additional options. You can:

- Click Save Reliability History and use the dialog box provided to select a save location and file name for a Reliability Monitor report. The report will contain complete details about the computer's stability, formatted using XML. You can view the report at any time in Internet Explorer by double-clicking the file. If you attach a report to an email message, you can send the report to someone who can help you with troubleshooting.

- Click View All Problem Reports to open the Problem Reports window and access a history of all identified problems and their status. Most problems have a status of Report Sent, Not Reported, More Data Required, or No Solution Available. To clear the history, click Clear All Problem Reports.

- Click Check For Solutions To All Problems to start automated diagnostics. When diagnostic testing is complete, Action Center shows any newly discovered problems and also provides solutions if known.

When you view all problem reports, the Problem Reports window lists problems that you can report by source, summary, date, and status. The status shows whether the problem has been sent. The status also shows when Microsoft needs more information from the general user community to resolve a problem, as well as when there is no solution available for a particular problem.

REAL WORLD Although it may seem rather odd that Windows lists problems as having no solution available, remember how diagnostics works. Diagnostics looks for specific types of Windows, application, and hardware failures. Some problems can be solved with updates and patches. Others, such as compatibility issues, may simply be a result of the way in which an application was written. Also remember that if a solution is available for a problem, the solution is shown in Action Center.

Regardless of the problem status, you can do something in the Problem Reports window that you can't always do in the Reliability Monitor window: You can right-click a problem and choose Check For Solution to re-check for a solution to a problem or Delete to remove a problem report from the history. You also can right-click a problem and choose View Solution to get more information about a problem that's been resolved or View Technical Details to get technical details about a problem.

Diagnosing and Resolving Problems with Troubleshooters

Windows 7 tracks failed installation, unresponsive conditions, and other problems in Action Center. Should an installation fail or an application become unresponsive, the built-in diagnostics adds an alert to Action Center and either provides a ready solution or allows you to check for a solution. Many other automated responses to problems are handled with troubleshooters.

The standard troubleshooters include:

- **Aero**   Detects and resolves problems preventing the computer from properly using Windows Aero.

- **Display Quality**   Detects and resolves problems affecting the quality of your computer's display.

- **Hardware And Devices**   Detects and resolves problems preventing the computer from properly using a device.

- **Homegroup**   Detects and resolves problems preventing the computer from sharing files in a homegroup.

- **Incoming Connections**   Detects and resolves problems preventing connections to your computer through Windows Firewall.

- **Internet Connections**   Detects and resolves problems preventing the computer from connecting to the Internet or an intranet.

- **Maintenance**   Performs routine maintenance if you don't.

- **Network Adapter**   Detects and resolves problems related to Ethernet, wireless, and other network adapters.

- **Performance**   Detects and resolves problems that are affecting the overall performance of the computer.

- **Playing Audio**   Detects and resolves problems preventing the computer from playing sound.

- **Power**   Detects and resolves problems that affect power management, sleep, hibernation, or resume.

- **Printer**   Detects and resolves problems preventing the computer from using a printer.

- **Program Compatibility**   Detects and resolves problems preventing a program from running on the computer.

- **Recording Audio**   Detects and resolves problems preventing the computer from recording sound.

- **Internet Explorer Performance**   Detects and resolves problems with add-ons, temporary files, and connections that are affecting Internet Explorer performance.

- **Internet Explorer Safety** Identifies issues with settings that could compromise the security of the computer and the safety of the user when browsing the web.

- **Windows Media** Detects and resolves problems preventing the computer from playing music or DVDs. Can also be used to reset Windows Media Player to its default settings.

- **Windows Update** Detects and resolves problems that are preventing you from updating the operating system.

If Windows PowerShell 2.0 is installed, related services are running, and troubleshooting is enabled, the troubleshooters can automatically detect and diagnose many common problems. If you suspect a problem that hasn't been detected, you can start a troubleshooter manually. To do this, follow these steps:

1. In Action Center, expand the Maintenance panel to determine whether there's a solution to your problem already listed. If a solution for your problem isn't listed, scroll down and click the Troubleshooting link.

2. As shown in Figure 7-4, links on the Troubleshooting page provide access to troubleshooters according to tasks you might want to perform. For example, you could click Run Programs Made For Previous Versions Of Windows to start the Program Compatibility troubleshooter.

3. If you don't see an appropriate task, click View All in the left pane to display a list of all available troubleshooters, and then click the troubleshooter you want to start.

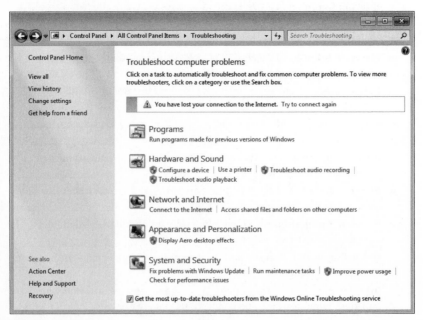

FIGURE 7-4 Resolving problems with the troubleshooters

NOTE As with Action Center, the Troubleshooting page alerts problems. For example, if your computer loses its connection t see an alert about this. Clicking Try To Connect Again starts t troubleshooter.

TIP By default, Windows looks for updates to troubleshooters online a automatically installs them. If you'd prefer not to do this, clear the Get The Mos. Up-To-Date Troubleshooters check box on the Troubleshooting page.

When you are working with the Troubleshooting page, note the View All, View History, and Change Settings options in the left pane. Selecting View All shows all available troubleshooters, listed alphabetically by name, description, location, category, and publisher. When a troubleshooter is listed as Local, the troubleshooter is available on your computer. When a troubleshooter is listed as Online, the troubleshooter is available online and will be downloaded and run each time you use it.

While you are working with the Troubleshooting page, don't overlook the View History option. The troubleshooting history shows you the troubleshooters run under your user account and when they were run. Click Include Troubleshooters That Were Run As An Administrator to view troubleshooters run with administrator privileges. More importantly, if you click an entry in the history, you can view and print a detailed troubleshooting report. The report shows the issues found and the fixes Windows tried, which can be as helpful as the troubleshooters themselves.

The Change Settings option on the Troubleshooting page is also useful, because it allows you to manage how troubleshooters are used. By default, Windows checks for routine maintenance issues and alerts you when a troubleshooter can help fix a problem. Windows also allows you and other users to browse for available troubleshooters online and begins troubleshooting immediately when you start a troubleshooter. Note that if you don't allow Windows to check online for new troubleshooters, your computer won't install updates for troubleshooters either.

TIP Each user who logs on to a computer has separate troubleshooting settings. In Group Policy, you can configure how automated troubleshooting and diagnostics work by making policy settings under \Computer Configuration\Administrative Templates\ System\Troubleshooting And Diagnostics.

Problems with hardware devices can be particularly difficult to resolve. If you suspect that a device isn't working properly, you can use Device Manager to verify whether the device is working properly. Start Device Manager by clicking Start, typing **devmgmt.msc**, and then pressing Enter; then examine the status of your computer's devices.

A device that is malfunctioning will have an error or warning icon. To view information about the error, right-click the device and then select Properties. For malfunctioning devices, the device properties will show an error status code and a suggested resolution for the code.

resolve many hardware device problems by reinstalling or updating the
driver. In Device Manager, right-click the device you want to work with, and
select Properties. On the Driver tab, click the Update Driver button and follow
prompts to reinstall or update the driver as appropriate.

You can also uninstall a driver and let Windows 7 reinstall the current version of
the driver files from the driver store. In Device Manager, right-click the device, and
then select Uninstall. Click OK in the Confirm Device Uninstall dialog box, but do not
select Delete The Driver Software For This Device. If reinstalling the device driver
doesn't work, check to make sure the device is properly inserted and connected.
You may need to disconnect and reconnect the device (while ensuring that the
computer is powered down and unplugged as appropriate and necessary).

If you are still unable to get the device to work properly, check the device
manufacturer's website for alternative versions of the device driver. You may find
that an older version of a device driver is more stable than the latest version.

Examining Resource Usage in Detail

Resource Monitor should be one of your tools of choice for performance tuning.
You use Resource Monitor to track resource usage on the computer. The information
provided is similar to Task Manager but more detailed.

You can open Resource Monitor by clicking Start, typing **perfmon.exe /res**,
and then pressing Enter. As Figure 7-5 shows, Resource Monitor provides resources
usage statistics for four categories:

- **CPU** Shows the current CPU utilization and the maximum CPU frequency
  (as related to processor idling). If you expand the CPU entry (by clicking the
  options button), you'll see a list of currently running executables by name,
  process ID (PID), description, status, number of threads used, current CPU
  utilization, and average CPU utilization.

- **Disk** Shows the number of kilobytes per second being read from or
  written to disk and the highest percentage of usage. If you expand the Disk
  entry (by clicking the options button), you'll see a list of currently running
  executables that are performing or have performed I/O operations by name,
  PID, file being read or written, average number of bytes being read per
  second, average number of bytes being written per second, total number of
  bytes being read and written per second, I/O priority, and the associated disk
  response time.

- **Network** Shows the current network bandwidth utilization in kilobytes and
  the percentage of total bandwidth utilization. If you expand the Network
  entry (by clicking the options button), you'll see a list of currently running
  executables that are transferring or have transferred data on the network
  by name, PID, computer or IP address being contacted, average number of
  bytes being sent per second, average number of bytes received per second,
  and total bytes sent or received per second.

- **Memory** Shows the current memory utilization and the number of hard faults occurring per second. If you expand the Memory entry (by clicking the Options button), you'll see a list of currently running executables by name, PID, hard faults per second, commit memory in KB, working set memory in KB, shareable memory in KB, and private (nonshareable) memory in KB.

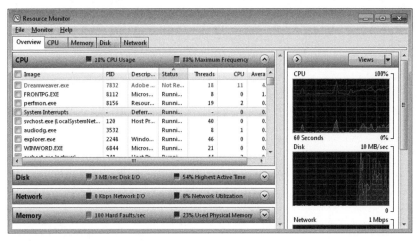

FIGURE 7-5 Tracking resource usage details

The Overview tab displays a general overview of all resource data for each of the four areas tracked. Expand the panels to see more details, or select the individual tabs to take a closer look at a specific area of resource usage.

One of the most useful features of Resource Monitor is the usage filter. On the Overview tab, you can filter by any combination of processes running on the computer simply by selecting the related checkboxes on the CPU panel. In the example shown in Figure 7-6, the data is filtered to focus on resource usage related to a specific application: Winword.exe. I've also added resource usage data for System processes.

After you've filtered the usage activity, the graphs highlight resource usage specific to the processes you've selected. As disk usage, network usage, and memory usage data are similarly filtered, you can see exactly what the selected processes are doing on your computer.

You can apply filters on the CPU, Memory, Disk, and Network tabs as well. The filters are global and affect what you see on all other tabs. Because of this, don't forget to remove filters you've applied if you want to examine other processes or view overall usage data again. To do this, simply clear the process check boxes that apply the filters.

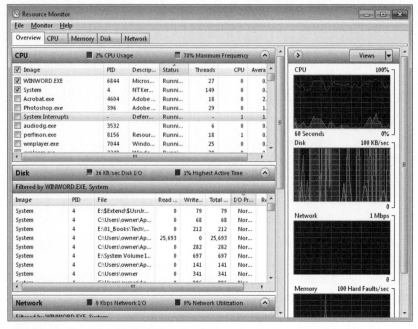

FIGURE 7-6 Getting more detailed information about resource usage

Recording and Analyzing Performance Data

You need to record performance data and analyze it to know what's really happening on your computer. Logging performance data isn't something you should do haphazardly. You should have a clear plan before you begin, and that plan should define specifically why you want to log performance data. For example, you might think that an application you are using has a memory leak that is causing your computer to perform poorly, and you could prove this by logging memory usage data while working with the application.

Logging Performance Data

Although Resource Monitor and Task Manager tell you what's happening on your computer, they don't delve deep enough to help you resolve every performance problem you'll encounter—this is where Performance Monitor is useful.

Performance Monitor graphs usage statistics for sets of performance parameters that you've selected for display. These performance parameters are referred to as *counters*. When you install certain applications on your computer, Performance Monitor might be updated with a set of counters for tracking related performance. Similarly, performance counters may be added when you install certain services and add-ons for Windows.

You can open Performance Monitor by clicking Start, typing **perfmon.msc**, and then pressing Enter. As Figure 7-7 shows, Performance Monitor creates a graph depicting the counters you're tracking.

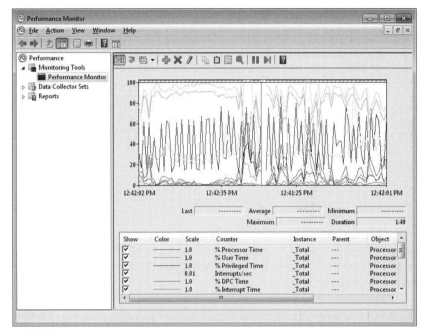

FIGURE 7-7 Analyzing performance metrics

Performance Monitor has several key features. A legend, displayed at the bottom of the details pane, shows the color and line style used for each counter. A value bar, displayed between the graph and the legend, shows values related to the counter you've selected in the graph or in the legend. A toolbar, displayed above the graph, provides the basic functions and options for working with Performance Monitor. Each toolbar button has a keyboard shortcut as well.

The toolbar buttons and their shortcut keys are as follows:

- **View Current Activity**   CTRL+T; switches the view so that current activity being logged is displayed.
- **View Log Data**   CTRL+L; switches the view so that data from a performance log can be replayed.
- **Change Graph Type**   CTRL+G; switches the view to toggle between bar graph, report list, and graph format.
- **Add**   CTRL+I; displays the Add Counters dialog box, which lets you add counters to track.

- **Delete** DELETE key; removes the currently selected counter so that it is no longer tracked.
- **Highlight** CTRL+H; highlights the currently selected counter with a white line so that it is more easy to see. To turn the Highlight function off, select the counter and press CTRL+H again.
- **Copy Properties** CTRL+C; creates a copy of the counter list, along with the individual configuration of each counter, and puts it on the Windows Clipboard as an Extensible Markup Language (XML) file.
- **Paste Counter List** CTRL+V; pastes a copied counter list into Performance Monitor so that it is used as the current counter set. If you saved a counter list to a file, you simply open the file, copy the contents of the file to the Clipboard, and then press CTRL+V in Performance Monitor to use that counter list.
- **Properties** CTRL+Q; displays the Properties dialog box for a select item.
- **Freeze Display** CTRL+F; freezes the display so that Performance Monitor no longer updates the performance information. Press CTRL+F again to resume sampling.
- **Update Data** CTRL+U; updates the display by one sampling interval. When you freeze the display, Performance Monitor still gathers performance information; it just doesn't update the display using the new information. To update the display while it is frozen, use this option.
- **Help** F1; displays the Performance Monitor Help information.

The graphing update interval is configurable, but it is set to 1 second by default. Because you'll often need to track many counters to identify a performance problem, you'll find that recording the performance data in a log and then analyzing the log data is typically the best approach. Performance Monitor also allows you to configure alerts that send messages when certain events occur.

To work effectively with Performance Monitor, you need to understand the difference between performance counters and performance objects. Performance counters represent the measurable properties of performance objects. A performance object can be a physical part of the operating system, such as the memory, the processor, or the paging file; a logical component, such as a logical disk or print queue; or a software element, such as a process or a thread.

Performance object instances represent single occurrences of performance objects. If a particular object has multiple instances, such as when a computer has multiple processors, you can use an object instance to track a specific occurrence of that object. You could also elect to track all instances of an object, such as when you want to monitor all processors on your computer.

The most common performance objects you'll want to monitor include:

- **Cache** Represents the file system cache, which is an area of physical memory that indicates application I/O activity.
- **LogicalDisk** Represents the logical volumes on your computer.

- **Memory** Represents memory performance for system cache (including pooled, paged memory and pooled, nonpaged memory), physical memory, and virtual memory.

- **Network Interface** Represents the network adapters configured on your computer.

- **Objects** Represents the number of events, processes, sections, semaphores, and threads on your computer.

- **Paging File** Represents page file current and peak usage.

- **PhysicalDisk** Represents hard disk read/write activity as well as data transfers, hard faults, and soft faults.

- **Print Queue** Represents print jobs, spooling, and print queue activity.

- **Process** Represents all processes running on your computer.

- **Processor** Represents processor idle time, idle states, usage, deferred procedure calls, and interrupts.

- **System** Represents system-level counters, including processes, threads, context switching of threads, file system control operations, system calls, and system uptime.

- **Thread** Represents all running threads and allows you to examine usage statistics for individual threads by process ID.

Each of these performance objects has a set of counters that can be tracked.

Choosing Counters to Monitor

Performance Monitor displays information only for counters that you're tracking. You'll find counters related to just about every logical and physical aspect of your computer. The easiest way to learn about these counters is to read the explanations available when you select a counter. To do this, start Performance Monitor, click Add on the toolbar, expand an object in the Available Counters list, and then select the Show Description check box. Now when you scroll through the list of counters for the selected object you'll see a detailed description of what the counter represents and how it can be used.

When you are configuring monitoring for a particular object, pay particular attention to the instances of that object that will be tracked. You can configure tracking for all instances of an object or for specific instances. For example, when you track the Physical Disk object, you have a choice of tracking all physical disk instances or specific physical disk instances. If you think a particular disk is going bad or experiencing other problems, you could monitor just that disk instance.

The two special instance types you should know are:

- **_Total** Tracks all instances of a counter in total, rather than separately. Use _Total to track the overall performance of all instances of a related counter. For example, if your computer has four processor cores, you could track their processor usage in total rather than separately for each processor core.

- **<All Instances>** Tracks all instances of a counter separately, rather than in total. Use <All Instances> to track all instances of a related counter separately. For example, if your computer has four processor cores, you could track processor usage individually for all processor instances.

Performance Monitor allows you to view performance data as graphed current data, line data, histogram data, and report data. By clicking View Current Activity on the toolbar or pressing Ctrl+T, you can be sure you are viewing a graph of current activity. You can switch between the view types by clicking Change Graph Type or pressing Ctrl+G.

In the Histogram Bar view, Performance Monitor represents the performance data by using a bar graph with the last sampling value for each counter graphed. The sizes of the bars within the graph are adjusted automatically based on the number of performance counters being tracked and can be adjusted to accommodate hundreds of counters, which is useful because it allows you to track multiple counters more easily than other views.

In the Report view, Performance Monitor represents the performance data in a report list format. In this view, objects and their counters are listed in alphabetical order and performance data is displayed numerically rather than graphed. If you are trying to determine specific performance values for many different counters, this is the best view to use because the actual values are always shown.

You can select counters to monitor by following these steps:

1. Click Add on the toolbar or press Ctrl+I to display the Add Counters dialog box (see Figure 7-8). Note that only administrators of the local computer and members of the local Performance Log users group can monitor performance data.

2. In the Available Counters section, performance objects are listed alphabetically. Click an object entry to select all related counters, or expand an object entry and then select individual counters by clicking them.

3. When you select an object or any of its counters, you see the related instances. Choose _Total to track all instances of a counter in total or <All Instances> to track all instances of a counter separately.

4. After you've selected an object or a group of counters for an object as well as the object instances, click Add to add the counters to the graph.

5. Repeat steps 2–3 to add other performance parameters. Click OK when you have finished and are ready to start graphing performance.

TIP Don't try to graph too many counters or counter instances at once. You'll make the display too difficult to read, and you'll use system resources.

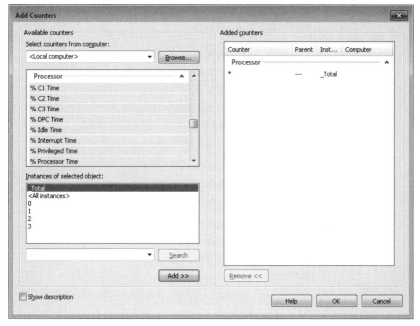

FIGURE 7-8 Adding counters to track

Identifying Performance Bottlenecks

The way your computer performs depends primarily on its memory configuration, its processors, its hard disks, and its networking components, each of which can act as a bottleneck that keeps your computer from performing at its best.

Your computer's memory is often the source of the biggest performance issues, and you should always rule out memory problems before examining other areas of the system. Because computers use both physical and virtual memory, look specifically at physical memory, caching, and virtual memory. Virtual memory is paged to disk and represented by the paging file. Look specifically at:

- Memory\Available Bytes
- Memory\Committed Bytes
- Memory\Commit Limit

If your computer has very little available memory, you might need to add memory. Generally, you want the available memory under normal usage conditions to be no less than 5 percent of the total physical memory on the computer. If your computer has a high ratio of committed bytes to total physical memory on the system, you might need to add memory as well. Generally, you want the committed bytes value to be no more than 75 percent of the total physical memory.

You should also look at memory page faults. To do this, track:

- Memory\Page Faults/sec
- Memory\Pages Input/sec
- Memory\Page Reads/sec

A page fault occurs when a process requests a page in memory and the operating system can't find it at the requested location. If the requested page is elsewhere in memory, the fault is called a *soft page fault*. If the requested page must be retrieved from disk, the fault is called a *hard page fault*. Most processors can handle large numbers of soft faults, but hard faults can cause performance problems.

Page Faults/sec is the overall rate at which the processor handles all types of page faults. Pages Input/sec is the total number of pages read from disk to resolve hard page faults. Page Reads/sec is the total disk reads needed to resolve hard page faults. Pages Input/sec will be greater than or equal to Page Reads/sec and can give you a good idea of your hard page fault rate. A high number of hard page faults could indicate that you need to increase the amount of memory or reduce the cache size on the computer.

For deeper problems, take a look at the page pool and the nonpaged pool by using Memory\Pool Paged Bytes and Memory\Pool Nonpaged Bytes. The paged pool is an area of system memory for objects that can be written to disk when they aren't used. The nonpaged pool is an area of system memory for objects that can't be written to disk.

If the size of the paged pool is large relative to the total amount of physical memory, you might need to add memory to your computer. If the size of the nonpaged pool is large relative to the total amount of virtual memory allocated, you might want to increase the virtual memory size.

Focus on your computer's processor after you have eliminated memory as a potential bottleneck source. If the computer's processors are the performance bottleneck, adding memory or faster drives won't resolve your performance problem. Instead, you might need to upgrade the processors to faster clock speeds or add processors. Look specifically at:

- System\Processor Queue Length
- Processor\% Processor Time

System\Processor Queue Length tracks the number of threads awaiting execution. These threads are queued in an area shared by all processors. If this counter has a sustained value of more than five threads per processor, you may need to upgrade or add processors.

Processor\% Processor Time tracks the percentage of time a processor is executing a nonidle thread. If the % Processor Time values are high and the network interface and disk I/O throughput rates are relatively low, you may need to upgrade or add processors.

Your computer's hard disks and networking components may be causes of bottlenecks as well. Accessing memory is much faster than reading from disk or retrieving data over a network. If your computer has to do a lot of reads and writes, whether to disk or over the network, its overall performance can be degraded. To reduce the amount of disk activity, you want the computer to manage memory very efficiently and page to disk only when necessary. See "Fine-Tuning Virtual Memory" in Chapter 8 for details.

If you've fine-tuned virtual memory and are still having problems, you may want to track counters related to disk I/O activity. Specifically, you should monitor:

- PhysicalDisk\% Disk Time
- PhysicalDisk\Disk Writes/sec
- PhysicalDisk\Disk Reads/sec
- PhysicalDisk\CurrentDisk Queue Length

PhysicalDisk\% Disk Time gives you a good picture of overall drive performance. Be sure to monitor % Disk Time for all hard disk drives on the computer, and use this counter in conjunction with Processor\% Processor Time and Network Interface Connection\Bytes Total/sec. If the % Disk Time value is high and the processor and network connection values aren't high, your computer's disk drives might be the source of a performance bottleneck.

The number of reads and writes per second reveals how much disk I/O activity there is. The disk queue length indicates the number of read or write requests that are waiting to be processed. Generally, you want very few waiting requests.

Although memory, processors, and hard disks have the biggest actual impact on performance, your perception about the speed and performance of your computer may be tied directly to its networking components. If your computer is still using a dial-up modem to connect to the Internet, your connection will be slow and transferring data will be painfully slow. Wireless connections can also seem very slow, especially if your network hasn't been upgraded to the latest and greatest high-speed wireless technologies.

Network latency can affect your experience. A long delay, or high degree of latency, between when a request is made and the time it's received can make your computer seem very slow. You can't do much about latency. It's a function of the type of connection and the route the request takes to your computer. On the other hand, the total capacity of your computer to handle requests and the amount of bandwidth available are factors you can control.

The capacity of your network card can be a limiting factor. Older computers may use 10/100 network cards instead of newer 100/1000 network cards. Someone might have configured a 100/1000 card for 100 Mbps, or the card might be configured for half duplex instead of full duplex. If you suspect a capacity problem with a network card, you should always check its configuration.

You can determine the throughput and current activity on your computer's network cards by using the following counters:

- Network Interface\Bytes Received/sec
- Network Interface\Bytes Sent/sec
- Network Interface\Bytes Total/sec
- Network Interface\Current Bandwidth

Compare these values in conjunction with PhysicalDisk\% Disk Time and Processor\% Processor Time. If the disk time and processor time values are low but the network values are very high, you might have a capacity problem. Solve the problem by optimizing the network card settings or by adding a network card. Remember that the hubs and routers on your network can also limit the networking speed. If your network card is 1000 Mbps and you want to operate at this speed, your network hubs and routers must support 1000 Mbps.

CHAPTER 8

Optimizing Performance Tips and Techniques

No discussion on optimizing Windows 7 is complete without a few final tips and techniques for boosting overall performance—and that's exactly what you'll find in this chapter. As you set out to use these tips and techniques, remember that your computer's performance is in your control. You'll need to fine-tune settings occasionally to keep things running smoothly. You'll need to perform maintenance as necessary. And you'll need to operate your computer while keeping in mind its relative performance ratings.

Optimizing Power Management Settings for Performance

Whether you have a laptop PC, tablet PC, or desktop PC, don't overlook the impact of power settings on your computer's performance. Power management settings are designed to save energy, but there is a direct tradeoff between power savings and performance.

Selecting and Using Power Plans

You use the Power Options page in Control Panel to manage your computer's power plans. Power plans are collections of power management settings that control power usage and consumption. A computer can have multiple power plans, but only one can be active at any particular time.

Open the Power Options page by clicking Start, typing**Powercfg.cpl** in the Search box on the Start menu, and then pressing Enter. Specify the power plan to use by clicking it in the Preferred Plans list. As shown in Figure 8-1, Windows 7 has three default power plans:

- **Balanced**   Balances energy usage and system performance. The processor speeds up when more resources are used and slows down when less are needed.

- **High Performance**   Optimizes the computer for performance while increasing energy usage. The plan ensures that you always have enough power for using graphics-intensive programs or playing multimedia games.

- **Power Saver**   Reduces power consumption while decreasing performance. The plan slows down the processor to conserve power.

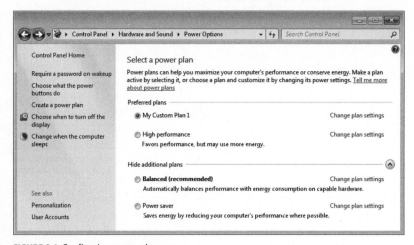

FIGURE 8-1 Configuring power plans

As Table 8-1 shows, power plans have basic and advanced settings. Basic settings control when a computer turns off its display and when it turns itself off. Advanced settings determine precisely whether and when power management components are shut down and how those components are configured for performance. The available advanced settings depend on the type of computer you are using.

TABLE 8-1 Power Plan Settings and Their Usage

BASIC SETTINGS	TURN OFF DISPLAY AFTER...	ENTER SLEEP MODE AFTER...
Balanced Plan	10 minutes inactivity	30 minutes inactivity
Power Saver Plan	5 minutes inactivity	15 minutes inactivity
High Performance Plan	15 minutes inactivity	Never

BASIC SETTINGS	TURN OFF DISPLAY AFTER...	ENTER SLEEP MODE AFTER...
ADVANCED SETTINGS	**DESCRIPTION**	**USAGE**
Battery\Reserve Battery Level	Determines the percentage of battery remaining that initiates reserve power mode.	Typical default is 7 percent, meaning enter reserve power mode when battery power reaches 7 percent remaining. A reserve level of 5 to 18 percent is often best.
Desktop Background Settings\Slide Show	Determines whether the slide show feature for the desktop background is available or paused.	Default is Available. Set to Paused to disable background slide shows on the desktop.
Display\Turn Off Display After	Determines whether and when a computer's display is turned off to conserve power.	Choosing Never disables this feature. Specific value in minutes sets inactive duration before the display is turned off.
Hard Disk\Turn Off Hard Disk After	Determines whether and when a computer's hard disk is turned off to conserve power.	Choosing Never (0) disables turning off the hard disk. Specific value in minutes sets inactive duration before hard disk is turned off.
Multimedia Settings\ When Playing Video	Determines the power optimization mode used when playing video.	Use Optimize Video Quality for best quality playback. Use Balanced for a balanced approach to adjusting playback quality to save power. Use Optimize Power Savings for active approach to adjusting playback quality to save power.

BASIC SETTINGS	TURN OFF DISPLAY AFTER...	ENTER SLEEP MODE AFTER...
Multimedia Settings\ When Sharing Media	Determines what the computer does when a device or another computer plays media from the computer.	Use Allow The Computer To Enter Away Mode to ensure computer will not enter sleep mode when sharing media. Use Allow The Computer To Sleep to allow the computer to enter sleep mode when inactive. Use Prevent Idling To Sleep to allow the computer to enter sleep mode only if set by user.
PCI Express\Link State Power Management	Determines the power saving mode to use with Peripheral Component Interconnect (PCI) Express devices connected to the computer.	Set this option to Off, Moderate Power Savings, or Maximum Power Savings.
Power Buttons And Lid\ Power Button Action	Specifies the action to take when someone pushes and holds the computer's power button.	Set this option to Do Nothing, Sleep, Hibernate, or Shutdown.
Power Buttons And Lid\ Sleep Button Action	Sets the default action for the sleep button. Use this setting to override the computer's default action.	Set this option to Do Nothing, Sleep, or Hibernate (as permitted).
Processor Power Management\Maximum Processor State	Sets a maximum or peak performance state for the computer's processor.	Lower to save power at a direct cost to responsiveness and computational speed. At 50 percent or below can cause a significant reduction in performance and responsiveness.

BASIC SETTINGS	TURN OFF DISPLAY AFTER...	ENTER SLEEP MODE AFTER...
Processor Power Management\Minimum Processor State	Sets a minimum performance state for the computer's processor.	Lower to save power at a direct cost to responsiveness and computational speed. 5 percent reduces responsiveness while offering substantial power savings. 50 percent helps to balance responsiveness and while moderately saving power. 100 percent maximize responsiveness but doesn't saving power.
Processor Power Management\System Cooling Policy	Determines whether the operating system increases the fan speed before slowing the processor.	Passive limitedly enables, and the processor may run hot. Active fully enables to help cool the processor.
PlanName\Require A Password On Wakeup	Determines whether a password is required when a computer wakes from sleep.	Set to Yes or No. With domain computers, controlled through Group Policy.
Sleep\Allow Hybrid Sleep	Specifies whether the computer uses hybrid sleep mode rather than the sleep mode used in earlier versions of Windows.	Set to On or Off. Hybrid sleep mode puts the computer in a low-power state until the user resumes using the computer. If the battery runs low, the computer hibernates.
Sleep\Allow Wake Timers	Determines whether timed events should be allowed to wake the computer from a sleep state.	Use Disable to prevent. Use Enable to allow.

BASIC SETTINGS	TURN OFF DISPLAY AFTER...	ENTER SLEEP MODE AFTER...
Sleep\Hibernate After	Determines whether and when a computer hibernates to conserve power.	Not normally used unless battery power runs low. Use Never to disable. Specific value in minutes sets inactive duration before the computer hibernates.
Sleep\Sleep After	Determines whether and when a computer enters a sleep state to conserve power.	Use Never to disable. Specific value in minutes sets inactive duration before the computer sleeps.
USB Settings\USB Selective Suspend Setting	Determines whether the USB selective suspend feature is available.	Use Disabled to turn off selective suspend. Use Enabled to allow selective suspend.
Wireless Adapter Settings\Power Saving Mode	Specifies the power saving mode to use with any wireless adapters connected to the computer.	Set to Maximum Performance, Low Power Saving, Medium Power Saving, or Maximum Power Saving.

REAL WORLD Differences in the advanced settings are what set the default power plans apart. As an example, the High Performance plan ensures performance by allowing the computer's processor to always run at 100 percent power consumption, whereas the Power Saver and the Balanced plans reduce energy consumption by configuring the processor to use a minimum power consumption rate of 5 percent and a maximum rate of 100 percent.

TIP In Group Policy, you can use a preference item to optimize power plans on computers throughout a domain. To configure power plan preferences for computers, expand Computer Configuration\Preferences\Control Panel Settings, and then select Power Options. To configure power plan preferences for users, expand User Configuration\Preferences\Control Panel Settings, and then select Power Options.

You can manage power plans from the command line by using the Power Configuration (Powercfg.exe) utility. Type **powercfg -l** at the command prompt list the power plans configured on a computer by name and globally unique identifier

(GUID). When you know the GUID for a power plan, you can work with it in a variety of ways:

- Type **powercfg –q** followed by a GUID to view the settings of the related plan.
- Type **powercfg –d** followed by a GUID to delete the related plan.
- Type **powercfg –s** followed by a GUID to set the related plan as the active plan.

If you want to see a complete list of all available parameters, type **powercfg /?** at the command prompt.

Creating and Optimizing Power Plans

In addition to the preferred power plans included with Windows 7, you can create power plans and optimize existing power plans as needed.

You can create a power plan by following these steps:

1. On the Power Options page, Click Create A Power Plan, and then select the default power plan that is closest to the type of plan you want to create.
2. In the Plan Name field, type a descriptive name for the plan; then click Next.
3. Use the Turn Off The Display drop-down list to specify whether or when the computer's display automatically turns off. Choose Never to disable this feature.
4. Use the Put The Computer To Sleep drop-down list to specify whether or when the computer automatically enters sleep mode. Choose Never to disable this feature.
5. Click Create to create the plan. On the Power Options page, the plan you created is selected by default.
6. Click Change Plan Settings for your new plan, and then click Change Advanced Power Settings.
7. Configure the advanced power options as appropriate, and then click OK to save your power plan.

You can optimize an existing power plan by following these steps:

1. On the Power Options page, select the power plan you want to configure, and then click Change Plan Settings.
2. Use the Turn Off Display drop-down list to specify whether or when the computer's display automatically turns off. Choose Never to disable this feature.
3. Use the Put The Computer To Sleep drop-down list to specify whether or when the computer automatically enters sleep mode. Choose Never to disable this feature.

4. To configure advanced options, click Change Advanced Power Settings, and then use the Power Options dialog box to configure your desired settings. Click OK to save any changes you've made.

5. Click Save Changes to update the power plan.

Resolving Power Problems That Are Affecting Performance

When it comes to power plans and power management, an aspect that's often overlooked is compatibility. To enter and exit sleep states, your computer must support either the S1 or S2 sleep state, also referred to as the Standby sleep states. Similarly, to use hybrid sleep and hibernate, your computer must support these states.

You can determine the sleep states supported by typing **powercfg -a** at the command prompt. This option lists the available sleep states on the computer and the reasons why a particular sleep state is not supported. If your computer does not support hybrid sleep, you should ensure that Sleep\Allow Hybrid Sleep is set to Off.

Every running application and every installed device must support power management for your computer to manage power and sleep states effectively. If an application is causing pause and resume problems, you can check with the developer for an update or newer version that fixes the problem. You can verify that the installed devices support power management appropriately by typing **powercfg -energy** at the command prompt. As shown in the following example, Powercfg provides details about each review step and also lets you know if problems were found.

```
powercfg -energy


Enabling tracing for 60 seconds...
Observing system behavior...
Analyzing trace data...
Analysis complete.

Energy efficiency problems were found.

8 Errors
8 Warnings
13 Informational

See C:\Users\owner\Documents\energy-report.html for more details.
```

When the Power Configuration utility finishes tracing and analyzing your computer, review the energy report generated by the utility in a web browser. As Figure 8-2 shows, the energy report begins with a header that provides information about your computer, including the version and release date of your computer's BIOS.

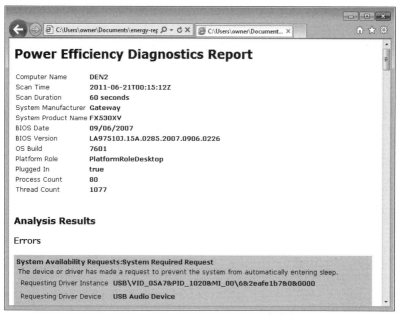

FIGURE 8-2 Reviewing the energy report

If your computer's BIOS hasn't been updated in a few years, you might want to check with the manufacturer to see if a newer version is available. Read the errors, warnings, and informational messages. If possible, take appropriate action to resolve errors. If a device has a power management issue, you may be able to resolve the problem by installing an updated driver or by changing the device's configuration options.

However, there are many caveats. Active devices, such as an audio device playing music, could prevent your computer from entering sleep mode during the analysis. This is normal, and success or failure is determined by the type of device and the power management settings.

The same device can generate a series of errors. For example, on my computer, a USB audio device prevented the system from automatically entering sleep mode during the analysis, and several other USB related errors were related to this device.

Other common errors you'll see relate to the display or to a particular device that may have had pending update requests during the testing. If there were pending requests for the display or any other device, these requests would prevent the computer from automatically powering off the display or the device, and also would prevent the computer from automatically entering a low-power sleep state.

You can get more information about pending requests made by device drivers by typing **powercfg –requests** at the command prompt. In the following example, a USB audio device has pending requests.

```
powercfg -requests


DISPLAY:
None.

SYSTEM:
[DRIVER] USB Audio Device
(USB\VID_05A7&PID_1020&MI_00\6&2eafe1b7&0&0000)
An audio stream is currently in use.

AWAYMODE:
None.
```

In this example, note the device identifier: USB\VID_05A7&PID_1020. Each error in the power report is associated with a specific device as well. To know for sure whether a device has a sleep and resume problem, you need to examine the detailed power support information available when you type **powercfg -devicequery all_devices_verbose** at a command prompt.

Because the information is so detailed, you'll want to redirect the command output to a text file, as shown in this example.

```
powercfg -devicequery all_devices_verbose > save.txt
```

Next, open the file in a text editor, such as Notepad, and search the file for the device identifier. Finally, review the output for the device to determine its power capabilities and supported sleep states.

Maintaining Performance with Updates

Your computer's performance is tied directly to the Windows components, hardware devices, and applications that are installed. Poor programming and coding problems can keep your computer from performing optimally. You can ensure that the most recent updates and hot fixes are applied to your computer by using Windows Update.

Windows Update allows your computer to automatically download and update operating system components and related programs. To take this process a step further, you can configure your computer to use Microsoft Update, which ensures that updates for Microsoft Office and other Microsoft products are updated as well.

Many applications from third-party vendors have update features as well. Use these update features whenever possible to keep installed applications up to date and performing optimally.

Fine-Tuning Automatic Updates

Windows Update integrates with Microsoft Update to ensure that the operating system and installed Microsoft applications stay up to date. When you install some Microsoft products, Microsoft Update is downloaded and installed automatically. For example, if you installed the Windows Live desktop programs, Microsoft Update is installed automatically as part of the setup process.

You can determine whether your computer is using Microsoft Update by following these steps:

1. Click Start, type **wuapp.exe**, and then press Enter.

2. If your computer is using Microsoft Update, you'll see the following message on the Windows Update page:

    You receive updates: For Windows and other products from Microsoft Update

If your computer isn't using Microsoft Update and you want to use this feature:

1. Click Get Updates For More Products on the Windows Update page. This accesses the Microsoft website in Internet Explorer.

2. After you read about Microsoft Update, scroll down, select I Accept The Terms Of Use, and then click Install.

While you are working with the Windows Update page in Control Panel, you should optimize the update settings. Click Change settings, and then specify whether and how updates should occur using the following techniques:

- To download and install updates automatically, select Install Updates Automatically and set the interval for installing updates. By default, your computer periodically checks for and downloads updates when you are connected to the Internet. However, updates are installed only on the specific days and times you set. If you shut down your computer after updates have been downloaded, the updates are installed automatically before the computer shuts down, unless you elect to shut down without installing updates.

- To ensure that recommended updates for device drivers included with the operating system and other optional updates are downloaded when they are available, select Give Me Recommended Updates The Same Way I Receive Important Updates. Recommended updates are not installed automatically. Instead, you are notified when recommended updates become available.

- To ensure that you receive updates for other Microsoft products and periodically check for new optional software from Microsoft, select Give Me Updates For Microsoft Products And Check For New Optional Microsoft Software When I Update Windows.

Save any changes you've made by clicking OK.

You can check for and install updates manually at any time by following these steps:

1. Click Start, type **wuapp.exe**, and then press Enter. As shown in Figure 8-3, statistics are provided regarding the most recent check for updates, the last time updates were installed, and the current update configuration.

2. Click Check For Updates. If updates are available, they are downloaded.

3. Links are provided that allow you to review each type of available update. Critical, important, and optional updates are listed separately. Click a link and then select the updates of that type to install, if any. Then, in the left pane, click the next type of update and select the updates of that type to install.

    NOTE If you are certain that you don't want to install an update, you can decline to install it and hide the update by right-clicking it and selecting Hide Update.

4. When you are ready to install all selected updates, click OK, and then click Install Updates. Remember that updates for hardware devices are listed as optional updates. Typically, you will want to install driver updates for your computer's hardware devices.

FIGURE 8-3 Checking for updates

Resolving Update Problems

Your computer may experience problems caused by installing updates. Although this happens rarely, it does happen. You can view a detailed update history and a list of both successful and failed updates by following these steps:

1. Click Start, type **wuapp.exe**, and then press Enter.

2. Click View Update History. On the View Update History page, updates listed with a Successful status were downloaded and installed. Updates listed with an Unsuccessful status were downloaded but failed to install.

3. To remove an update while accessing the View Update History page, click Installed Updates. Then, on the Installed Updates page, right-click the update that you do not want and select Uninstall.

If you decline an update that you later want to install, you can restore the update so that you can install it by completing these steps:

1. Click Start, type **wuapp.exe**, and then press Enter.

2. Click Restore Hidden Updates. On the Restore Hidden Updates page, select an update you want to install, and then click Restore.

3. Click Back to display the main Windows Update page. Important and Optional Updates links allow you to review each type of available update. Click a link to access the Select Updates To Install Page.

4. Locate the critical, important, or optional update you previously declined to install, select it, click OK, and then click Install Updates.

Optimizing Performance: Final Tune-up Suggestions

Throughout this book, and in this chapter particularly, I've discussed techniques for optimizing your computer's performance. If you've been following along, you've fine-tuned just about every aspect of your computer. Now let's look at a few additional areas for the final tune-up, including:

- Services and features
- Virtual memory
- Data execution prevention
- System cache
- Hard disk drives

The sections that follow discuss each in turn.

Disabling Unnecessary Services and Features

System services provide critical functions for your computer. However, unnecessary services use system resources and are a potential source of security problems. If your computer is running a service you don't need, such as Worldwide Web Publishing Service, you can disable the service or remove the related feature.

Typically, you should start by disabling services rather than uninstalling components. This way, if you disable a service that was actually needed, you can easily re-enable it if necessary. If you have local administrator privileges on your computer, you can disable a service by following these steps:

1. Start the Computer Management console by clicking Start, typing **compmgmt.msc**, and then pressing Enter.

2. Select the Services node, right-click the service you want to configure, and then choose Properties. On the General tab, select Disabled in the Startup Type drop-down list.

3. Disabling a service doesn't stop a running service; it only prevents the service from being started the next time the computer is booted. As necessary, click Stop on the General tab in the Properties dialog box, and then click OK.

You can turn off Windows features by following these steps:

1. Click Start, type **OptionalFeatures.exe**, and then press Enter.

2. Clear the check box for the feature you want to turn off, and then click OK. You may need to restart your computer. If prompted to do so, save your work and then click Restart.

Fine-Tuning Virtual Memory

Your computer uses virtual memory to extend the amount of available RAM. Virtual memory is written to disk through a process called paging. The operating system can access the paging file, Pagefile.sys, from disk when needed in place of physical memory. By default, Windows 7 creates an initial paging file automatically for the drive containing the operating system and does not use other drives for paging.

Typically, you don't need to put a paging file on multiple disks, because doing so won't necessarily boost performance, but you may want to put the paging file on your highest-performing drive. Windows 7 does a much better job than its predecessors do of automatically managing virtual memory. Typically, Windows 7 allocates virtual memory at least as large as the total physical memory installed on the computer. This approach reduces fragmentation of the paging file and helps to maintain overall read/write performance.

If you want to manually manage virtual memory, you'll typically want to use a fixed virtual memory size. You fix the size of the virtual memory by setting the initial size and the maximum size to the same value, and this in turn prevents fragmentation of the paging file. For most computers, I recommend setting the total paging file size so that it's twice the size of the physical RAM. However, if your computer has more than 4 GB of RAM, you'll probably want to set the paging file size so that it's approximately 1.5 times the size of the physical memory. Here are examples:

- On a computer with 2048 MB of RAM, you would ensure that the paging file size is at least 4096 MB.

- On a computer with 6144 MB of RAM, you would ensure that the paging file size is at least 9216 MB.

You can view the current virtual memory configuration by completing the following steps:

1. Click Start, type **SystemPropertiesPerformance**, and then press Enter. This opens the Performance Options dialog box.

2. On the Advanced tab, click Change to display the Virtual Memory dialog box.

Figure 8-4 shows an automatically managed paging file configuration on the left and a manually set paging file configuration on the right. Note the following:

- **Automatically Manage Paging File Size For All Drives** Controls whether the operating system manages the paging file.

- **Drive [Volume Label] And Paging File Size (MB)** Shows the current configuration of virtual memory. Each disk volume is listed with its associated paging file (if any). The initial and maximum size values of the related paging file are shown as well.

- **Paging File Size For Each Drive** Provides information on the currently selected drive and allows you to set its paging file size. Space Available indicates how much space is available on the drive.

- **Total Paging File Size For All Drives** Shows the minimum, recommended, and currently allocated virtual memory.

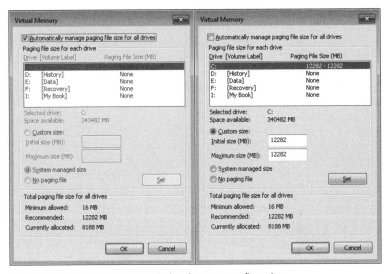

FIGURE 8-4 Checking your computer's virtual memory configuration

You can configure virtual memory by completing the following steps:

1. Open the Virtual Memory dialog box and do one of the following:

   - If you want Windows to manage virtual memory, select Automatically Manage Paging File Size For All Drives, click OK, and skip steps 2–4.

   - If you want to configure virtual memory manually, clear Automatically Manage Paging File Size For All Drives and continue with step 2.

2. In the Drive box, click the disk volume you want to work with, and then select Custom Size.

3. Enter an initial size and a maximum size for the paging file on the selected disk. Click Set to save the changes.

4. Repeat steps 2 and 3 for each disk volume you want to have a paging file.

5. Click OK. If prompted to overwrite an existing Pagefile.sys file, click Yes.

6. If you updated the settings for a paging file that is currently in use, you will be prompted that you need to restart the system for the changes to take effect. Click OK.

7. Click OK twice to close the open dialog boxes. A prompt asks if you want to restart the system. Click Restart.

Fine-Tuning Data Execution Prevention

Windows 7 uses Data Execution Prevention (DEP) to mark memory locations used by applications as nonexecutable unless the location explicitly contains executable code. If an application attempts to execute code from a memory page marked as nonexecutable, the processor can raise an exception and prevent it from executing. DEP is designed to thwart malware from inserting itself into areas of memory and in this way protects your computer.

DEP is implemented in hardware and software. Hardware-based DEP is the most effective because it encompasses any program or service running on the computer. Software-based DEP is less effective because it typically works best only when protecting Windows programs and services. Although DEP is designed to protect your computer, the feature can affect performance.

> **REAL WORLD** Windows 32-bit versions support DEP as implemented originally by Advanced Micro Devices Inc. (AMD) processors that provide the no-execute page-protection (NX) processor feature. Such processors support the related instructions and must be running in Physical Address Extension (PAE) mode. Windows 64-bit versions also support the NX processor feature but do not need to be running in PAE mode.

You can determine whether your computer supports hardware-based DEP by completing the following steps:

1. Click Start, type **SystemPropertiesDataExecutionPrevention**, and then press Enter. This opens the Performance Options dialog box.

2. If your computer supports hardware-based DEP, the lower portion of the Data Execution Prevention tab appears as shown in Figure 8-5.

After accessing the Data Execution Prevention tab, you can manage the way DEP works by using these options:

- **Turn On DEP For Essential Windows Programs And Services Only** Enables DEP only for services, programs, and components of the operating system. This is the default and recommended setting for computers that support execution protection and are configured appropriately.

- **Turn On DEP For All Programs And Services Except Those I Select** Enables DEP for services, programs, and components of the operating system and all other programs and services the computer is running.

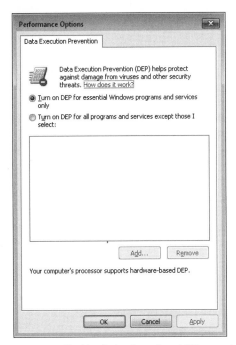

FIGURE 8-5 Checking for hardware-based DEP support

Some programs won't work with or will become unstable with DEP, and you may find that you have to add exceptions when you enable DEP for all programs. Click Add to specify programs that should run without execution protection. Execution protection will work for all programs except those you have listed.

Enhancing Performance with ReadyBoost

Non-critical kernel memory is paged to virtual memory, as part of the system cache. Although virtual memory is useful, reading from and writing to a disk is significantly slower than reading from and writing to physical memory (RAM). To reduce the performance impact related to reading and writing the system cache from virtual memory, you can configure your computer to use Windows ReadyBoost.

Windows ReadyBoost lets you extend the disk-caching capabilities of the computer's main memory to a USB flash device that has at least 256 MB of high-speed flash memory. You cannot configure this feature on removable hard drives or USB flash devices with poorly performing flash memory.

The operating system uses the flash memory primarily for caching that uses random input/output and small, sequential input/output rather than large, sequential input/output. This is because the flash memory is better suited to random I/O and small, sequential input/output than large, sequential I/O. By caching data on the USB flash device instead of your computer's disk drives, Windows makes faster random reads, which boosts overall performance because it's up to 1,000 percent faster than reading from physical disk drives.

REAL WORLD As a safeguard, Windows 7 adds protection to prevent the sudden removal of a USB flash device from crashing the computer and to prevent reading of any sensitive data written to the flash device. Windows 7 eliminates the potential for data loss when removing a flash device by writing to the paging file on disk first and then copying data to the flash device. Windows 7 encrypts all data written to a flash device to prevent reading of sensitive data on another computer.

To enable Windows ReadyBoost, insert a USB flash device into a USB 2.0 or higher port. The AutoPlay dialog box should appear automatically; click Speed Up My System. If the AutoPlay dialog box does not appear, click Start, click Computer, right-click the device, and then select Properties.

If the flash device is not compatible, you'll see a warning about this, as shown in the first example in Figure 8-6; you won't be able to turn on ReadyBoost. If the flash device is compatible, as shown in the second example in the figure, you can configure ReadyBoost.

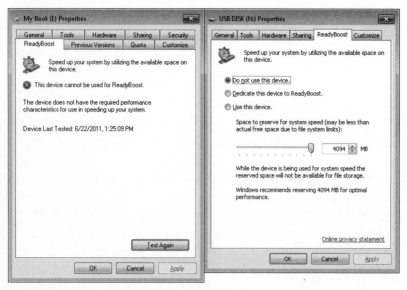

FIGURE 8-6 Enabling and configuring Windows ReadyBoost

You can reserve from 230 MB to 4094 MB of flash memory for ReadyBoost. I recommend using as much as possible. To automatically reserve the maximum amount of space for ReadyBoost, select Dedicate This Device To ReadyBoost. Otherwise, select Use This Device, and then use the Space To Reserve For System Speed slider or combo box to set the amount of space to use with ReadyBoost. When you click OK, Windows 7 extends the computer's physical memory to the device.

NOTE Choosing either setting option doesn't prevent you from writing files to the device. Your choice simply determines the amount of space to reserve for ReadyBoost. If you reserve less than the total amount of space available, the free space can be used for files and data.

You can safely remove a USB flash device that uses ReadyBoost at any time. Simply right-click the USB flash device in the Computer window, and then choose Eject or Safely Remove.

Cleaning Up Your Disk Drives

Your computer may slow down as its disks fill to capacity, because it uses available space to write the paging file and other temporary files it needs to use. Ideally, you should ensure that any disk used by the operating system to write system files has at least 15 percent free space. Otherwise, you may start to notice that your computer is not as responsive as it should be.

You can clean up your computer's disks by using Disk Cleanup, which locates temporary files and allows you to remove them. Temporary files you can delete in this way include:

- Copies of network files designated for offline use.
- Dump files created because of STOP errors.
- Files that have been deleted from the computer but not yet purged from the Recycle Bin.
- Hibernation files used when your computer enters sleep mode.
- Log files and other temporary files that Office uses.
- Log files that Windows created during setup.
- Previous Windows installations saved under Windows.old.
- Programs downloaded for use by your browser.
- Temporary copies of recently used offline files
- Temporary files stored in the Temp folder by applications.
- Temporary files used for error reporting and checking for solutions to problems.
- Temporary Internet files stored to support browser caching of pages.
- Thumbnails of pictures, videos, and documents created by Windows.

Although you can delete most temporary files without hesitation, you may want to retain:

- Setup log files, if you are still configuring your computer after installation.
- Previous Windows installations, if you haven't saved user data or other necessary data they may contain.
- Dump files related to unresolved STOP errors, as they may be needed for troubleshooting.
- Thumbnails, because Windows would need to create them the next time you access folders.

Clean up your computer's disk by completing the following steps:

1. Click Start, type **Disk Cleanup**, and then press Enter.

2. Select the disk that you want to clean up. When you click OK, Disk Cleanup examines the selected drive, looking for temporary files that can be deleted and files that are candidates for compression. The more files on the drive, the longer the search process takes.

3. When Disk Cleanup is complete, a list of temporary files that can be deleted appears as shown in Figure 8-7. Add system files to the cleanup list by clicking Clean Up System Files, selecting the primary system drive, and then clicking OK. The primary system disk is the disk with the Windows logo.

4. By default, only a few types of temporary files are selected. As appropriate, review the other types of temporary files that you can delete and mark them for deletion by selecting them.

5. Click OK. When prompted to confirm, click Yes.

FIGURE 8-7 Reviewing files to delete using Disk Cleanup

Checking Your Disks for Errors

Your computer is constantly reading from and writing to its primary disk. If a particular sector or cluster on a disk is damaged or otherwise cannot be written to, your computer will experience problems whenever it tries to read from or write to this sector or cluster. Although the operating system and drive controllers help to mitigate and correct disk problems, they can't prevent and correct all disk problems. Occasionally errors occur, and you need to check your computer's disk periodically to correct these errors.

You can check for and correct disk errors by using Check Disk, which has three operating modes:

- **Checkonly** Performs a three-phase check of the selected disk and notes any errors found. Faster than the other modes. Useful for checking the primary disk without having to restart the computer.

NOTE With NTFS: Phase 1 verifies file records. Phase 2 verifies index entries in the file system table. Phase 3 verifies security descriptors and journal sequencing.

- **Check and fix** Performs a three-phase check of the selected disk followed by a repair of any errors found in the file system. Runs a check of the selected disk and attempts to fix any errors found in the file system.

- **Check, fix, and recover** Performs a multi-phase check of the selected disk. Also attempts to fix any errors found in the file system and recover bad sectors.

A disk cannot be active during the check and repair process. A primary disk will be marked for analysis and repair during the next restart. You can dismount any other disk if it is in use or mark it for analysis and repair during the next restart.

You can check a disk by following these steps:

1. Click Start, and then click Computer. Under Hard Disk Drives, right-click the drive you want to check, and then select Properties.

2. On the Tools tab, click Check Now. This displays the Check Disk dialog box, shown in Figure 8-8.

3. Use the options provided to set the operating mode for Check Disk. For a check only, clear both options and then click OK. For a check and fix, select Automatically Fix File System Errors. For a check, fix, and recover, select both Automatically Fix File System Errors and Scan For And Attempt Recovery Of Bad Sectors.

FIGURE 8-8 Checking a disk for errors

4. Click Start, and then do one of the following:

- With a primary disk, Check Disk displays a prompt that asks whether you want to schedule the disk to be checked the next time you restart the computer. Schedule this check.

- With other disks, Check Disk displays a prompt if the disk is in use. If you want to dismount the disk and check it, click Force A Dismount. Otherwise, click Cancel and schedule the disk to be checked the next time you restart the computer when prompted.

NOTE Dismounting a disk gives the operating system exclusive control. Be sure to save your current work before you dismount a disk.

Optimizing Disk Performance

Another problem that causes disk drives to perform poorly is fragmentation. Fragmentation occurs when a file can't be written to a single contiguous area on the disk and the operating system must write a single file to several areas on the disk. Not only does this slow down the write process, it also slows down the read process.

To reduce fragmentation, Windows 7 uses Disk Defragmenter to defragment disks automatically. Windows 7 runs a Disk Defragmenter scheduled task at 1:00 A.M. every Wednesday by default. If the computer is on at the scheduled runtime and idle for at least 3 minutes, automatic defragmentation occurs. Otherwise, automatic defragmentation occurs the next time the computer is on and idle for at least 3 minutes.

Your computer being idle is an important pre-condition of the scheduled task. If you start using your computer, the task will stop and wait for the processor to become idle again before starting or continuing defragmentation. The task will run for up to three days, waiting for idle time to complete its work.

You can manage the settings for automatic defragmentation by following these steps:

1. Click Start, and then click Computer. Under Hard Disk Drives, right-click a hard drive and select Properties.

2. On the Tools tab, click Defragment Now. This displays the Disk Defragmenter dialog box, shown in Figure 8-9.

3. Cancel automatic defragmentation by clicking Configure Schedule, and then clearing Run On A Schedule. Click OK, then Close. Skip the remaining steps.

4. Otherwise, with Run On A Schedule selected, select the frequency, day, time, and disks to set the desired run schedule. For example, you might want to schedule automatic defragmentation to occur every Monday at 9:00 A.M. during your yoga class.

5. Click OK, then Close to save your settings.

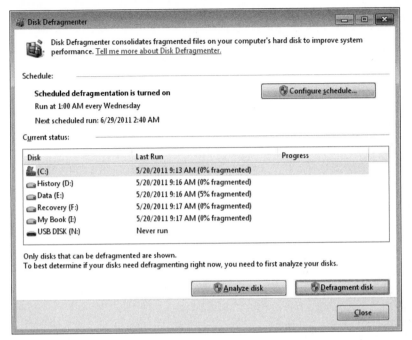

FIGURE 8-9 Configuring automatic defragmentation

When you access Disk Defragmenter, the last runtime and next runtime are listed. If your computer hasn't been automatically defragmented in several weeks or months, you can defragment a disk manually by completing the following steps:

1. Click Start, and then click Computer. Under Hard Disk Drives, right-click a hard drive and select Properties.

2. On the Tools tab, click Defragment Now.

3. In the Disk Defragmenter dialog box, select the disk to defragment, and then click Defragment Disk.

Defragmentation can take several hours. You can click Stop Operation at any time to stop defragmentation.

Firmware Interface Options

THE WAY YOUR COMPUTER'S firmware interface operates and the tasks it performs depend on the type of firmware interface and the type of central processing unit (CPU). Most computers built today have CPUs based on either 32-bit x86 architecture or 64-bit extensions to this architecture, referred to as x64 architecture.

Table A-1 shows a composite of firmware interface options I've encountered in my workplace. When you are working with a desktop computer, you'll likely find options that serve similar purposes, and you may want to customize these options for the way you want your computer to work. Because there are few standards and conventions among firmware interface manufacturers, firmware interface options with similar purposes can have very different labels.

TABLE A-1 Options in Firmware

OPTION	VALUES	DESCRIPTION
AC Recovery	Off, On, Last	Specifies the mode of operation if a power loss occurs. The system will stay off, power on, or resume the last state.
ACPI Suspend State	S1 State, S3 State	Specifies the suspend mode to use as S1 (maintains hardware and processor contexts) or S3 (discards contexts and only maintains system memory).
After Power Failure	Stay Off, Last State, Power On	Specifies the mode of operation if a power loss occurs. The system will stay off, resume the last state, or power on.

OPTION	VALUES	DESCRIPTION
ATA/IDE Mode	Enhanced, Legacy	Configures SATA to be in enhanced (native) or legacy mode.
Audio	Enable, Disable	Enables or disables the on-board audio device.
Auto Power On	Off, Everyday, Weekdays	Specifies whether and when the system powers on automatically. Select Off to turn the feature off. Select Everyday to power on automatically every day of the week. Select Weekdays to power on automatically Monday through Friday.
Auto Power Time	[Time]	If Auto Power On is enabled, use this option to set the time to automatically power on, such as 7:30 A.M.
Boot To Hard Disk Drive	Enable, Disable	Enables or disables booting to disk drives.
Boot To Network	Enable, Disable	Enables or disables booting to the network.
Boot To Optical Devices	Enable, Disable	Enables or disables booting to optical devices.
Boot To Removable Devices	Enable, Disable	Enables or disables booting to removable devices.
Clear Event Log	Enable, Disable	When enabled, clears the hardware event log.
Configure SATA	IDE, RAID, AHCI	Configures SATA to use the corresponding type.
Diskette Controller	Disable, Enable, Automatic	Enables or disables the floppy disk controller.
Diskette Write Protection	Enable, Disable	Enables or disables floppy disk write protection.
Display Setup Prompt	On, Off	Determines whether the prompt to access Setup is displayed.
EIST	Enable, Disable	Specifies whether the processor will use Enhanced Intel SpeedStep Technology (EIST).

OPTION	VALUES	DESCRIPTION
Enter Intel AMT BX Setup	Enable, Disable	Enables or disables use of and access to Intel's automated management functionality.
Event Logging	Enable, Disable	Enables or disables hardware event logging.
Execute Disable	On, Off	Controls whether Data Execution Prevention (DEP) memory protection technology is on or off.
Fast Boot	On, Off	Specifies whether fast boot is on or off. With fast boot on, the computer skips certain self-tests in the boot process to boot more quickly.
Floppy Type	1.44 MB, 2.88 MB	Sets the floppy media capacity.
Front Fan Speed		Shows the speed of the front fan.
Hard Disk Pre-Delay	[#]	Specifies the amount of time in seconds that the firmware will wait to detect hard disk drives.
HDD Acoustic Mode	Bypass, Quiet, Suggested, Performance	Optimizes drive performance and acoustic noise level based on the selection: Bypass (do nothing; required for older drives), Quiet (slower but quieter), Suggested (allow drive manufacturer to select the mode), Performance (faster but possibly noisier).
HPET	Enable, Disable	Enables or disables support for the High Precision Event Timer.
Integrated Audio	On, Off	Determines whether the integrated audio device is on or off.
Integrated NIC	On, Off	Determines whether the integrated network adapter is on or off.
Intel Quick Resume Technology	Enable, Disable	Enables or disables Intel Quick Resume.

OPTION	VALUES	DESCRIPTION
Internal temp		Shows the operating temperature of the motherboard.
Keyboard Errors	Report, Do Not Report	Controls whether keyboard errors are displayed when the system boots. Use Report to display keyboard errors.
Mark Events As Read	Enable, Disable	When enabled, marks events as read.
MAX CPUID Value Limit	Enable, Disable	Disable for legacy operating systems that cannot support CPUs with extended CPUID functions.
Mode	Output only, Bidirectional, EPP	Determines the peripheral mode.
Multiple CPU Core	On, Off	Specifies whether the processor will have multiple cores enabled. To turn on support for multiple cores, choose On. Otherwise, choose Off.
Numlock On/Off	On, Off	Sets the default state for the Numlock key as on or off.
On-board 1394	Enable, Disable	Enables or disables the on-board IEEE 1394 adapter.
On-board LAN	Enable, Disable	Enables or disables the on-board network adapter.
OS Install	On, Off	Specifies whether the operating system install mode is on. Some operating systems will not install when there is more than 2 gigabytes (GB) of system memory. Turn this on to allow installation.
Parallel Port	Enable, Disable	Determines whether the parallel port is available.
PCI Express Compliance Test Pattern	Enable, Disable	Enables or disables compliance testing for PCI Express devices.
PCI Latency Timer	[Time]	Sets the latency timer used with PCI Express devices.

OPTION	VALUES	DESCRIPTION
POST Hotkeys	Setup & Boot, Setup, Boot	Controls which options are available at startup: Setup & Boot (displays both F2=Setup and F12=Boot menu messages), Setup (displays the F2=Setup message), Boot (displays the F12=Boot menu message), None (displays neither message).
Primary Video	PCI, PEG	Specifies which video controller will be the primary video controller: PCI (use the PCI video controller), PEG (use the PCI Express Graphics video controller).
Primary Video Adapter	[Type]	Sets the type of the primary video adapter.
Processor Fan Speed		Shows the speed of the processor fan.
Processor Thermal Margin		Shows the acceptable operating temperatures for the processor.
Rear Fan Speed		Shows the speed of the rear fan.
S.M.A.R.T.	Enable, Disable	Enables or disables self-monitoring analysis and reporting technology.
SATA Operation	RAID Autodetect / AHCI, RAID Autodetect / ATA, RAID On, Combo	Configures the integrated hard drive controller: AHCI (use RAID if signed drives; otherwise use AHCI), ATA (use RAID if signed drives; otherwise use ATA), RAID On (always use RAID), Combo (use SATA/PATA combination mode).
Serial Port	Enable, Disable	Determines whether the serial port is available.
SpeedStep	Enable, Disable	Specifies whether the processor will use EIST.
Suspend Mode	S3, S1	Specifies the suspend mode to use as S3 or S1.
System Fan Control	Enable, Disable	Enables or disables control of the system fan.

OPTION	VALUES	DESCRIPTION
Trusted Platform Module	Enable, Disable	Enables or disables the on-board TPM.
USB 3.0	Enable, Disable	Enables or disables support for USB 3.0.
USB 2.0	Enable, Disable	Enables or disables support for USB 2.0.
USB Boot	Enable, Disable	Enables or disables booting to USB devices.
USB Legacy	Enable, Disable	Enables or disables support for legacy USB.
USB Mass Storage Emulation Type	Auto, All Removable, All Fixed Disk, Size	Sets the emulation type for USB drives as automatic, removable media emulation, fixed disk emulation, or emulation based on the size of the USB drive.
Use Automatic Mode	Enable, Disable	Determines whether the automatic drive mode is used.
View Event Log		When selected, displays the hardware event log.
Voltage ratings		When selected, shows the acceptable voltage ratings.
Wake On LAN From S5	Stay Off, Power On	Specifies the action taken when the system power is off and an ACPI power management wakeup event occurs.
ZIP Emulation Type	Floppy, Hard Disk	Sets the emulation type to use for ZIP drives.

Index

Symbols and Numbers

About the Author

WILLIAM R. STANEK (*http://www.williamstanek.com/*) has more than 20 years of hands-on experience with advanced programming and development. He is a leading technology expert, an award-winning author, and a pretty-darn-good instructional trainer. Over the years, his practical advice has helped millions of programmers, developers, and network engineers all over the world. His current and forthcoming books include *Exchange Server 2010 Administrator's Pocket Consultant, Windows PowerShell 2.0 Administrator's Pocket Consultant,* and *Windows Server 2008 Inside Out.*

William has been involved in the commercial Internet community since 1991. His core business and technology experience comes from more than 11 years of military service. He has substantial experience in developing server technology, encryption, and Internet solutions. He has written many technical white papers and training courses on a wide variety of topics. He frequently serves as a subject matter expert and consultant.

William has an MS with distinction in information systems and a BS in computer science, magna cum laude. He is proud to have served in the Persian Gulf War as a combat crewmember on an electronic warfare aircraft. He flew on numerous combat missions into Iraq and was awarded nine medals for his wartime service, including one of the United States of America's highest flying honors, the Air Force Distinguished Flying Cross. Currently, he resides in the Pacific Northwest with his wife and children.

William recently rediscovered his love of the great outdoors. When he's not writing, he can be found hiking, biking, backpacking, traveling, or trekking in search of adventure with his family!

Find William on Facebook at *http://www.facebook.com/wstanek*. Follow William on Twitter at *http://twitter.com/WilliamStanek*.

What do you think of this book?

We want to hear from you!
To participate in a brief online survey, please visit:

microsoft.com/learning/booksurvey

Tell us how well this book meets your needs—what works effectively, and what we can do better. Your feedback will help us continually improve our books and learning resources for you.

Thank you in advance for your input!